The Other Civil War

ALSO BY HOWARD ZINN

Voices of a People's History of the United States, second edition, with Anthony Arnove (2004, 2009)

The Zinn Reader: Writings on Disobedience and Democracy, second edition (2009)

A Young People's History of the United States, adapted by Rebecca Stefoff (2008, 2009)

The Unraveling of the Bush Presidency (2007)

A Power Governments Cannot Suppress (2007)

The People Speak (2006)

Original Zinn: Conversations on History and Politics with David Barsamian (2006)

Artists in Time of War (2003)

Passionate Declarations: Essays on War and Justice (2003)

You Can't Be Neutral on a Moving Train: A Personal History of Our Times, second edition (2002)

Terrorism and War, with Anthony Arnove (2002)

Emma: A Play (2002)

A People's History of the United States: 1492–Present, updated edition (2001)

Three Strikes: Miners, Musicians, Salesgirls, and the Fighting Spirit of Labor's Last Century, with Dana Frank and Robin D.G. Kelley (2001)

Howard Zinn on War (2001)

Howard Zinn on History (2001)

La otra historia de los Estados Unidos (2001)

Marx in Soho: A Play on History (1999)

The Future History: Interviews with David Barsamian (1999)

Failure to Quit: Reflections of an Optimistic Historian (1993, 2002)

The Politics of History, second edition (1990)

Justice: Eyewitness Accounts (1977, 2002)

Postwar America: 1945–1971 (1973, 2002)

Disobedience and Democracy: Nine Fallacies of Law and Order (1968, 2002)

Vietnam: The Logic of Withdrawal (1967, 2002)

SNCC: The New Abolitionists (1964, 2002)

The Southern Mystique (1964, 2002)

LaGuardia in Congress (1959)

The Other Civil War

Slavery and Struggle in Civil War America

excepted from *A People's History of the United States*

Howard Zinn

HARPER ● PERENNIAL

NEW YORK ● LONDON ● TORONTO ● SYDNEY ● NEW DELHI ● AUCKLAND

HARPER PERENNIAL

FIRST EDITION

Designed by Michael P. Correy

Library of Congress Cataloging-in-Publication Data is avail-able upon request.

ISBN 978-0-06-207900-8

11 12 13 14 15   OV/RRD   10 9 8 7 6 5 4 3 2 1

Contents

The Other Civil War

FOREWORD

I'm delighted that HarperCollins asked me to preface this book on the Civil War taken from Howard Zinn's massive bestseller *A People's History of the United States*. Personally I'm pleased, because Zinn's blurb for *Lies My Teacher Told Me* helped it become a bestseller. The larger reason for my delight is the effect that *People's History* has had on legions of readers. Since the success of *Lies*, I have been giving talks around the United States lamenting how badly U.S. history is taught and leading workshops on how to do better. Often, audience members come up afterward to tell me that their high school history teacher was different: "She assigned us *People's History* as well as the regular textbook, and her course was interesting." The result, often enough, was to inspire students to lives of critical reading and thoughtful acting about social issues—in short, to citizenship.

Owing in part to extensive connections Zinn forged with African-Americans during his years teaching at Spelman College, *The Other Civil War* supplies a stellar introduction to the difficult topic of slavery. Zinn makes judicious use of primary sources, such as the "slave narratives" taken down by the WPA in the 1930s, as well as secondary works by historians like Eugene Genovese. This book provides an understanding of slaves as real people—hurting, constrained, doing the best they could under terrible circumstances. Zinn also shows that a society built on slavery must always live in fear as a garrison state.

In keeping with the nature of his undertaking, Zinn offers much less material about the upper class. Therefore he doesn't say much about why the South left the Union. This is understandable, because the elite was quite clear about its motivation; there should be no issue to address. Unfortunately, because high school history textbooks cover secession particularly badly, Americans today often misunderstand why the South left the Union. Kindly allow me to add a corrective here to the wrong information you may have learned in high school.

Since 1998, I have been asking audiences, "Why did the Southern states secede?" Always I get four answers:

(1) slavery
(2) states' rights
(3) the election of Lincoln
(4) tariffs and taxes (or issues about tariffs and taxes)

I then ask for a vote. To my surprise, region makes no difference. From central Florida to North Dakota, states' rights regularly draws 55 to 75 percent of the votes. Slavery usually receives about 20

percent. The election of Lincoln gets only a hand-
ful—2 to 5 percent. Tariffs and taxes varies from 10
to 20 percent, depending largely on how many votes
go to states' rights.

Two of these answers—states' rights and tariffs
and taxes—are dramatically wrong. As the secession statements collected in *The Confederate and Neo-
Confederate Reader* show, Confederates were against
states' rights. In its key document, "Declaration of
the Immediate Causes Which Induce and Justify
the Secession of South Carolina from the Federal
Union," the first state to secede spelled out precisely
the reasons that prompted South Carolina to want
out.

> Maine, New Hampshire, Vermont, Massachusetts,
> Connecticut, Rhode Island, New York, Pennsyl-
> vania, Illinois, Indiana, Michigan, Wisconsin and
> Iowa, have enacted laws which either nullify the
> Acts of Congress or render useless any attempt to
> execute them. In many of these States the fugitive
> is discharged from service or labor claimed.

South Carolina went on to attack New York for
no longer allowing "slavery transit"—such as slave
owners bringing an enslaved cook along to New York
City when vacationing there. New England upset
South Carolina by letting African-Americans vote,
even though the right to vote in the United States
was a state matter until the fourteenth and fifteenth
Constitutional amendments were adopted two eras
later, during Reconstruction. South Carolina was
further upset that Northern states "have permit-

ted open establishment among them of [abolitionist] societies." Other states echoed these grievances. In short, Southern states seceded for slavery, not states' rights. Nor did they complain about tariffs. Why would they? The South had helped write the tariff under which the United States was functioning.

Zinn writes, "The clash was not over slavery as a moral institution—most Northerners did not care enough about slavery to make" war over it. He is right that the North did not make war to end slavery but to hold the nation together. Most white Southerners, on the other hand, were outraged at abolitionists' moral attacks on slavery. They indeed cared enough about the institution—and its allied ideology of white supremacy—to secede, knowing that war would likely result. Thus the clash was over slavery, so far as the white South was concerned, and over disunion, so far as the North was concerned.

As early as 1862, however, U.S. army units were marching into formation singing "Battle Cry of Freedom." Dynamics of the war made emancipation inevitable, so long as the United States won. Army units, especially in the West and in Sherman's campaign through Georgia, came to rely on the black infrastructure for food, water, directions, and information as to where the Confederates were. The sights and sounds of slavery—whipping posts, scarred backs, sorrowful people seeking lost kin—made their impression too. Furthermore, white units found their survival depending upon the performance of the United States Colored Troops next to them—and black units fought well. Rapidly, most U.S. soldiers became abolitionists. Gradually, other Northerners became abolitionists too, as they read letters from their relatives in the armed forces and talked with people back from the front. Zinn's portrayal of emancipation is conspiratorial, asserting that "the political and economic needs of the business elite of the North" directed the process and later clamped limits on the extent of black freedom. In reality, the events of 1860–65 spiraled out of control. No elite was in charge. Besides, the elite was split. Many Northern business and banking men had ties to Southern slave owners and were Democrats, even Copperheads, during the war. They hardly directed Republican policy.

To Howard Zinn's credit, he quotes the bulk of Abraham Lincoln's letter of August 22, 1862, to Horace Greeley's *New York Tribune*. This letter is the favorite Lincoln quotation of authors; it is used by fifteen of the eighteen textbooks I surveyed. But they excerpt only these two sentences:

If I could save the Union without freeing *any* slave, I would do it; and if I could save it by freeing all the slaves, I would do it; and if I could save it by freeing some and leaving others alone, I would also do that. What I do about slavery and the colored race I do because I believe it helps to save this Union; and what I forbear, I forbear because I do not believe it would help to save the Union.

Thus they present a Lincoln unconcerned about slavery, concerned only with saving the nation. Zinn gives readers what Lincoln wrote next:

I have here stated my purpose according to my
view of official duty, and I intend no modification
of my oft-expressed personal wish that all men,
everywhere, could be free.

Zinn also shows the racism of the North and
Lincoln's need to hold the loyalty of Kentucky and
Missouri. What's more, Zinn questions Lincoln's
views on slavery. He points to the inadequacies of
the Emancipation Proclamation and notes that
even with its limitations, it was too radical for most
Northern voters and cost the Republicans dearly in
the November 1862 election. Lincoln always understood that if he got too far ahead of the electorate, he
would cease to have followers.

Turning to Reconstruction, Zinn again uses quo-
tations from the time to present African-Americans
as they really were—working, voting, trying to start
families with no material legacy from their enslaved
past. Zinn then adds something no "regular" textbook does: an extensive account of the class struggle
in the North as well as the South. His detailed de-
piction of the sordid city streets and dangerous industrial working conditions of the 1870s comes as
a revelation to today's suburban high school and
college students. The resulting labor unrest in
1876–77 coincided with the end of Reconstruction.
These twin defeats for the working poor provide a
moving end to this account of the Civil War era.

This history is important, even in the second de-
cade of a new millennium. Tourists still venerate slave
owners and make pilgrimages to their mansions in
Natchez and Charleston, not grasping the reality of

slavery. Politicians in Georgia, Texas, and Alaska suggest we seriously consider secession, misunderstanding and romanticizing the first secession. Judges order an end to affirmative action, not realizing the discrimination that pervaded the North and South after 1877 and especially after 1890. Investment bankers and CEOs receive ever higher multiples of the average income earned by factory workers and store clerks, not understanding how the astounding inequalities of the 1870s hurt our nation. America still has a lot to learn from Howard Zinn.

James W. Loewen
November 23, 2010

1

Slavery Without Submission,
Emancipation Without Freedom

The United States government's support of slavery was based on an overpowering practicality. In 1790, a thousand tons of cotton were being produced every year in the South. By 1860, it was a million tons. In the same period, 500,000 slaves grew to 4 million. A system harried by slave rebellions and conspiracies (Gabriel Prosser, 1800; Denmark Vesey, 1822; Nat Turner, 1831) developed a network of controls in the southern states, backed by the laws, courts, armed forces, and race prejudice of the nation's political leaders.

It would take either a full-scale slave rebellion or a full-scale war to end such a deeply entrenched system. If a rebellion, it might get out of hand, and turn its ferocity beyond slavery to the most successful system of capitalist enrichment in the world. If a war, those who made the war would organize its consequences. Hence, it was Abraham Lincoln who freed the slaves, not John Brown. In 1859, John Brown was hanged, with federal complicity, for attempting to do by small-scale violence what Lincoln would do by large-scale violence several years later—end slavery.

With slavery abolished by order of the government—true, a government pushed hard to do so, by blacks, free and slave, and by white abolitionists—its end could be orchestrated so as to set limits to emancipation. Liberation from the top would go only so far as the interests of the dominant groups permitted. If carried further by the momentum of war, the rhetoric of a crusade, it could be pulled back to a safer position. Thus, while the ending of slavery led to a reconstruction of national politics and economics, it was not a radical reconstruction, but a safe one—in fact, a profitable one.

The plantation system, based on tobacco growing in Virginia, North Carolina, and Kentucky, and rice in South Carolina, expanded into lush new cotton lands in Georgia, Alabama, Mississippi—and needed more slaves. But slave importation became illegal in 1808. Therefore, "from the beginning, the law went unenforced," says John Hope Franklin *(From Slavery to Freedom)*. "The long, unprotected coast, the certain markets, and the prospects of huge profits were too much for the American merchants and they yielded to the temptation. . . ." He estimates that perhaps 250,000 slaves were imported illegally before the Civil War.

How can slavery be described? Perhaps not at all by those who have not experienced it. The 1932 edition of a best-selling textbook by two northern liberal historians saw slavery as perhaps the Negro's "necessary transition to civilization." Economists or cliometricians (statistical historians) have tried to assess slavery by estimating how much money was spent on slaves for food and medical care. But can this describe the reality of slavery as it was to a human being who lived inside it? Are the *conditions* of slavery as important as the *existence* of slavery?

John Little, a former slave, wrote:

They say slaves are happy, because they laugh, and are merry. I myself and three or four others, have received two hundred lashes in the day, and had our feet in fetters; yet, at night, we would sing and dance, and make others laugh at the rattling of our chains. Happy men we must have been! We did it to keep down trouble, and to keep our hearts from being completely broken: that is as true as the gospel! Just look at it,—must not we have been very happy? Yet I have done it myself— I have cut capers in chains.

A record of deaths kept in a plantation journal (now in the University of North Carolina Archives) lists the ages and cause of death of all those who died on the plantation between 1850 and 1855. Of the thirty-two who died in that period, only four reached the age of sixty, four reached the age of fifty, seven died in their forties, seven died in their twenties or thirties, and nine died before they were five years old.

But can statistics record what it meant for families to be torn apart, when a master, for profit, sold a husband or a wife, a son or a daughter? In 1858, a slave named Abream Scriven was sold by his master, and wrote to his wife: "Give my love to my father and mother and tell them good Bye for me, and if we Shall not meet in this world I hope to meet in heaven."

One recent book on slavery (Robert Fogel and Stanley Engerman, *Time on the Cross*) looks at whippings in 1840–1842 on the Barrow plantation in Louisiana with two hundred slaves: "The records show that over the course of two years a total of 160 whippings were administered, an average of 0.7 whippings per hand per year. About half the hands were not whipped at all during the period." One could also say: "Half of all slaves were whipped." That has a different ring. That figure (0.7 per hand per year) shows whipping was infrequent for any individual. But looked at another way, once every four or five days, *some* slave was whipped.

Barrow as a plantation owner, according to his biographer, was no worse than the average. He spent money on clothing for his slaves, gave them holiday celebrations, built a dance hall for them. He also built a jail and "was constantly devising ingenious punishments, for he realized that uncertainty was an important aid in keeping his gangs well in hand."

The whippings, the punishments, were work disciplines. Still, Herbert Gutman *(Slavery and the Numbers Game)* finds, dissecting Fogel and

Engerman's statistics, "Over all, four in five cotton pickers engaged in one or more disorderly acts in 1840–41. . . . As a group, a slightly higher percentage of women than men committed seven or more disorderly acts." Thus, Gutman disputes the argument of Fogel and Engerman that the Barrow plantation slaves became "devoted, hardworking responsible slaves who identified their fortunes with the fortunes of their masters."

Slave revolts in the United States were not as frequent or as large-scale as those in the Caribbean islands or in South America. Probably the largest slave revolt in the United States took place near New Orleans in 1811. Four to five hundred slaves gathered after a rising at the plantation of a Major Andry. Armed with cane knives, axes, and clubs, they wounded Andry, killed his son, and began marching from plantation to plantation, their numbers growing. They were attacked by U.S. army and militia forces; sixty-six were killed on the spot, and sixteen were tried and shot by a firing squad.

The conspiracy of Denmark Vesey, himself a free Negro, was thwarted before it could be carried out in 1822. The plan was to burn Charleston, South Carolina, then the sixth-largest city in the nation, and to initiate a general revolt of slaves in the area. Several witnesses said thousands of blacks were implicated in one way or another. Blacks had made about 250 pike heads and bayonets and over three hundred daggers, according to Herbert Aptheker's account. But the plan was betrayed, and thirty-five blacks, including Vesey, were hanged. The trial record itself, published in Charleston, was ordered destroyed soon after publication, as too dangerous for slaves to see.

Nat Turner's rebellion in Southampton County, Virginia, in the summer of 1831, threw the slave-holding South into a panic, and then into a determined effort to bolster the security of the slave system. Turner, claiming religious visions, gathered about seventy slaves, who went on a rampage from plantation to plantation, murdering at least fifty-five men, women, and children. They gathered supporters, but were captured as their ammunition ran out. Turner and perhaps eighteen others were hanged.

Did such rebellions set back the cause of emancipation, as some moderate abolitionists claimed at the time? An answer was given in 1845 by James Hammond, a supporter of slavery:

> But if your course was wholly different—If you distilled nectar from your lips and discoursed sweetest music. . . . do you imagine you could prevail on us to give up a thousand millions of dollars in the value of our slaves, and a thousand millions of dollars more in the depreciation of our lands . . . ?

The slaveowner understood this, and prepared. Henry Tragle (*The Southampton Slave Revolt of 1831*), says:

> In 1831, Virginia was an armed and garrisoned state. . . . With a total population of 1,211,405, the

State of Virginia was able to field a militia force of 101,488 men, including cavalry, artillery, grenadiers, riflemen, and light infantry! It is true that this was a "paper army" in some ways, in that the county regiments were not fully armed and equipped, but it is still an astonishing commentary on the state of the public mind of the time. During a period when neither the State nor the nation faced any sort of exterior threat, we find that Virginia felt the need to maintain a security force roughly ten percent of the total number of its inhabitants: black and white, male and female, slave and free!

Rebellion, though rare, was a constant fear among slaveowners. Ulrich Phillips, a southerner whose *American Negro Slavery* is a classic study, wrote:

A great number of southerners at all times held the firm belief that the negro population was so docile, so little cohesive, and in the main so friendly toward the whites and so contented that a disastrous insurrection by them would be impossible. But on the whole, there was much greater anxiety abroad in the land than historians have told of. . . .

Eugene Genovese, in his comprehensive study of slavery, *Roll, Jordan, Roll,* sees a record of "simultaneous accommodation and resistance to slavery." The resistance included stealing property, sabotage and slowness, killing overseers and masters, burning down plantation buildings, running away. Even the accommodation "breathed a critical spirit and disguised subversive actions." Most of this resistance, Genovese stresses, fell short of organized insurrection, but its significance for masters and slaves was enormous.

Running away was much more realistic than armed insurrection. During the 1850s about a thousand slaves a year escaped into the North, Canada, and Mexico. Thousands ran away for short periods. And this despite the terror facing the runaway. The dogs used in tracking fugitives "bit, tore, mutilated, and if not pulled off in time, killed their prey," Genovese says.

Harriet Tubman, born into slavery, her head injured by an overseer when she was fifteen, made her way to freedom alone as a young woman, then became the most famous conductor on the Underground Railroad. She made nineteen dangerous trips back and forth, often disguised, escorting more than three hundred slaves to freedom, always carrying a pistol, telling the fugitives, "You'll be free or die." She expressed her philosophy: "There was one of two things I had a right to, liberty or death; if I could not have one, I would have the other; for no man should take me alive. . . ."

One overseer told a visitor to his plantation that "some negroes are determined never to let a white man whip them and will resist you, when you attempt it; of course you must kill them in that case."

One form of resistance was not to work so hard. W.E.B. DuBois wrote, in *The Gift of Black Folk:*

As a tropical product with a sensuous receptivity

to the beauty of the world, he was not as easily reduced to be the mechanical draft-horse which the northern European laborer became. He . . . tended to work as the results pleased him and refused to work or sought to refuse when he did not find the spiritual returns adequate; thus he was easily accused of laziness and driven as a slave when in truth he brought to modern manual labor a renewed valuation of life.

Ulrich Phillips described "truancy," "absconding," "vacations without leave," and "resolute efforts to escape from bondage altogether." He also described collective actions:

Occasionally, however, a squad would strike in a body as a protest against severities. An episode of this sort was recounted in a letter of a Georgia overseer to his absent employer: "Sir, I write you a few lines in order to let you know that six of your hands has left the plantation—every man but Jack. They displeased me with their work and I give some of them a few lashes, Tom with the rest. On Wednesday morning, they were missing."

The instances where poor whites helped slaves were not frequent, but sufficient to show the need for setting one group against the other. Genovese says:

The slaveholders . . . suspected that non-slaveholders would encourage slave disobedience and even rebellion, not so much out of sympathy for the blacks as out of hatred for the rich planters and resentment of their own poverty. White men sometimes were linked to slave insurrectionary plots, and each such incident rekindled fears.

This helps explain the stern police measures against whites who fraternized with blacks.

Herbert Aptheker quotes a report to the governor of Virginia on a slave conspiracy in 1802: "I have just received information that three white persons are concerned in the plot; and they have arms and ammunition concealed under their houses, and were to give aid when the negroes should begin." One of the conspiring slaves said that it was "the common run of poor white people" who were involved.

In return, blacks helped whites in need. One black runaway told of a slave woman who had received fifty lashes of the whip for giving food to a white neighbor who was poor and sick.

When the Brunswick canal was built in Georgia, the black slaves and white Irish workers were segregated, the excuse being that they would do violence against one another. That may well have been true, but Fanny Kemble, the famous actress and wife of a planter, wrote in her journal:

But the Irish are not only quarrelers, and rioters, and fighters, and drinkers, and despisers of niggers—they are a passionate, impulsive, warm-hearted, generous people, much given to powerful indignations, which break out suddenly when not compelled to smoulder sullenly—pestilent sympathizers too, and with a sufficient dose of

American atmospheric air in their lungs, properly mixed with a right proportion of ardent spirits, there is no saying but what they might actually take to sympathy with the slaves, and I leave you to judge of the possible consequences. You perceive, I am sure, that they can by no means be allowed to work together on the Brunswick Canal.

The need for slave control led to an ingenious device, paying poor whites—themselves so troublesome for two hundred years of southern history—to be overseers of black labor and therefore buffers for black hatred.

Religion was used for control. A book consulted by many planters was the *Cotton Plantation Record and Account Book,* which gave these instructions to overseers: "You will find that an hour devoted every Sabbath morning to their moral and religious instruction would prove a great aid to you in bringing about a better state of things amongst the Negroes."

As for black preachers, as Genovese puts it, "they had to speak a language defiant enough to hold the high-spirited among their flock but neither so inflammatory as to rouse them to battles they could not win nor so ominous as to arouse the ire of ruling powers." Practicality decided: "The slave communities, embedded as they were among numerically preponderant and militarily powerful whites, counseled a strategy of patience, of acceptance of what could not be helped, of a dogged effort to keep the black community alive and healthy—a strategy of survival that, like its African prototype, above all said yes to life in this world."

It was once thought that slavery had destroyed the black family. And so the black condition was blamed on family frailty, rather than on poverty and prejudice. Blacks without families, helpless, lacking kinship and identity, would have no will to resist. But interviews with ex-slaves, done in the 1930s by the Federal Writers Project of the New Deal for the Library of Congress, showed a different story, which George Rawick summarizes *(From Sundown to Sunup)*:

> The slave community acted like a generalized extended kinship system in which all adults looked after all children and there was little division between "my children for whom I'm responsible" and "your children for whom you're responsible." . . . A kind of family relationship in which older children have great responsibility for caring for younger siblings is obviously more functionally integrative and useful for slaves than the pattern of sibling rivalry and often dislike that frequently comes out of contemporary middle-class nuclear families composed of highly individuated persons. . . . Indeed, the activity of the slaves in creating patterns of family life that were functionally integrative did more than merely prevent the destruction of personality. . . . It was part and parcel, as we shall see, of the social process out of which came black pride, black identity, black culture, the black community, and black rebellion in America.

Old letters and records dug out by historian Herbert Gutman *(The Black Family in Slavery and Free-*

dom) show the stubborn resistance of the slave family to pressures of disintegration. A woman wrote to her son from whom she had been separated for twenty years: "I long to see you in my old age . . . Now my dear son I pray you to come and see your dear old Mother. . . . I love you Cato you love your Mother— You are my only son. . . ."

And a man wrote to his wife, sold away from him with their children: "Send me some of the children's hair in a separate paper with their names on the paper. . . . I had rather anything to had happened to me most than ever to have been parted from you and the children. . . . Laura I do love you the same. . . ."

Going through records of slave marriages, Gutman found how high was the incidence of marriage among slave men and women, and how stable these marriages were. He studied the remarkably complete records kept on one South Carolina plantation. He found a birth register of two hundred slaves extending from the eighteenth century to just before the Civil War; it showed stable kin networks, steadfast marriages, unusual fidelity, and resistance to forced marriages.

Slaves hung on determinedly to their selves, to their love of family, their wholeness. A shoemaker on the South Carolina Sea Islands expressed this in his own way: "I'se lost an arm but it hasn't gone out of my brains."

This family solidarity carried into the twentieth century. The remarkable southern black farmer Nate Shaw recalled that when his sister died, leaving three children, his father proposed sharing their care, and he responded:

That suits me, Papa. . . . Let's handle em like this: don't get the two little boys, the youngest ones, off at your house and the oldest one be at my house and we hold these little boys apart and won't bring em to see one another. I'll bring the little boy that I keep, the oldest one, around to your home amongst the other two. And you forward the others to my house and let em grow up knowin that they are brothers. Don't keep em separated in a way that they'll forget about one another. Don't do that, Papa.

Also insisting on the strength of blacks even under slavery, Lawrence Levine *(Black Culture and Black Consciousness)* gives a picture of a rich culture among slaves, a complex mixture of adaptation and rebellion, through the creativity of stories and songs:

We raise de wheat,
Dey gib us de corn;
We bake de bread,
Dey gib us de crust.
We sif de meal,
Dey gib us de huss;
We peel de meat,
Dey gib us de skin;
And dat's de way
Dey take us in;
We skim de pot,
Dey gib us de liquor,
An say dat's good enough for nigger.

There was mockery. The poet William Cullen Bryant, after attending a corn shucking in 1843 in South Carolina, told of slave dances turned into a pretended military parade, "a sort of burlesque of our militia trainings. . . ."

Spirituals often had double meanings. The song "O Canaan, sweet Canaan, I am bound for the land of Canaan" often meant that slaves meant to get to the North, their Canaan. During the Civil War, slaves began to make up new spirituals with bolder messages: "Before I'd be a slave, I'd be buried in my grave, and go home to my Lord and be saved." And the spiritual "Many Thousand Go":

No more peck o' corn for me, no more, no more,
No more driver's lash for me, no more, no more. . . .

Levine refers to slave resistance as "pre-political," expressed in countless ways in daily life and culture. Music, magic, art, religion, were all ways, he says, for slaves to hold on to their humanity.

While southern slaves held on, free blacks in the North (there were about 130,000 in 1830, about 200,000 in 1850) agitated for the abolition of slavery. In 1829, David Walker, son of a slave, but born free in North Carolina, moved to Boston, where he sold old clothes. The pamphlet he wrote and printed, *Walker's Appeal,* became widely known. It infuriated southern slaveholders; Georgia offered a reward of $10,000 to anyone who would deliver Walker alive, and $1,000 to anyone who would kill him. It is not hard to understand why when you read his *Appeal.*

There was no slavery in history, even that of the
Israelites in Egypt, worse than the slavery of the
black man in America, Walker said. " . . . show me a
page of history, either sacred or profane, on which a
verse can be found, which maintains, that the Egyp-
tians heaped the insupportable insult upon the children of Israel, by telling them that they were not of
the human family."

Walker was scathing to his fellow blacks who
would assimilate: "I would wish, candidly . . . to be
understood, that I would not give a pinch of snuff to
be married to any white person I ever saw in all the
days of my life."

Blacks must fight for their freedom, he said:

Let our enemies go on with their butcheries, and
at once fill up their cup. Never make an attempt
to gain our freedom or natural right from under
our cruel oppressors and murderers, until you see
your way clear—when that hour arrives and you
move, be not afraid or dismayed. . . . God has been
pleased to give us two eyes, two hands, two feet,
and some sense in our heads as well as they. They
have no more right to hold us in slavery than we
have to hold them. . . . Our sufferings will come
to an end, in spite of all the Americans this side of
eternity. Then we will want all the learning and
talents among ourselves, and perhaps more, to
govern ourselves.—"Every dog must have its day,"
the American's is coming to an end.

One summer day in 1830, David Walker was
found dead near the doorway of his shop in Boston.

Some born in slavery acted out the unfulfilled desire of millions. Frederick Douglass, a slave, sent to Baltimore to work as a servant and as a laborer in the shipyard, somehow learned to read and write, and at twenty-one, in the year 1838, escaped to the North, where he became the most famous black man of his time, as lecturer, newspaper editor, writer. In his autobiography, *Narrative of the Life of Frederick Douglass,* he recalled his first childhood thoughts about his condition:

> Why am I a slave? Why are some people slaves, and others masters? Was there ever a time when this was not so? How did the relation commence?
>
> Once, however, engaged in the inquiry, I was not very long in finding out the true solution of the matter. It was not color, but crime, not God, but man, that afforded the true explanation of the existence of slavery; nor was I long in finding out another important truth, viz: what man can make, man can unmake. . . .
>
> I distinctly remember being, even then, most strongly impressed with the idea of being a free man some day. This cheering assurance was an inborn dream of my human nature—a constant menace to slavery—and one which all the powers of slavery were unable to silence or extinguish.

The Fugitive Slave Act passed in 1850 was a concession to the southern states in return for the admission of the Mexican war territories (California, especially) into the Union as nonslave states. The Act made it easy for slaveowners to recapture ex-slaves

or simply to pick up blacks they claimed had run
away. Northern blacks organized resistance to the
Fugitive Slave Act, denouncing President Fillmore,
who signed it, and Senator Daniel Webster, who supported it. One of these was J. W. Loguen, son of a
slave mother and her white owner. He had escaped
to freedom on his master's horse, gone to college,
and was now a minister in Syracuse, New York. He
spoke to a meeting in that city in 1850:

> The time has come to change the tones of submis-
> sion into tones of defiance—and to tell Mr. Fill-
> more and Mr. Webster, if they propose to execute
> this measure upon us, to send on their blood-
> hounds. . . . I received my freedom from Heaven,
> and with it came the command to defend my title
> to it. . . . I don't respect this law—I don't fear it—I
> won't obey it! It outlaws me, and I outlaw it. . . . I
> will not live a slave, and if force is employed to re-
> enslave me, I shall make preparations to meet the
> crisis as becomes a man. . . . Your decision tonight
> in favor of resistance will give vent to the spirit of
> liberty, and it will break the bands of party, and
> shout for joy all over the North. . . . Heaven knows
> that this act of noble daring will break out some-
> where—and may God grant that Syracuse be the
> honored spot, whence it shall send an earthquake
> voice through the land!

The following year, Syracuse had its chance. A
runaway slave named Jerry was captured and put
on trial. A crowd used crowbars and a battering ram
to break into the courthouse, defying marshals with

drawn guns, and set Jerry free.

Loguen made his home in Syracuse a major station on the Underground Railroad. It was said that he helped 1,500 slaves on their way to Canada. His memoir of slavery came to the attention of his former mistress, and she wrote to him, asking him either to return or to send her $1,000 in compensation. Loguen's reply to her was printed in the abolitionist newspaper, *The Liberator:*

> Mrs. Sarah Logue. . . . You say you have offers to buy me, and that you shall sell me if I do not send you $1000, and in the same breath and almost in the same sentence, you say, "You know we raised you as we did our own children." Woman, did you raise your own children for the market? Did you raise them for the whipping post? Did you raise them to be driven off, bound to a coffle in chains? . . . Shame on you!
>
> But you say I am a thief, because I took the old mare along with me. Have you got to learn that I had a better right to the old mare, as you call her, than Manasseth Logue had to me? Is it a greater sin for me to steal his horse, than it was for him to rob my mother's cradle, and steal me? . . . Have you got to learn that human rights are mutual and reciprocal, and if you take my liberty and life, you forfeit your own liberty and life? Before God and high heaven, is there a law for one man which is not a law for every other man?
>
> If you or any other speculator on my body and rights, wish to know how I regard my rights, they need but come here, and lay their hands on me to enslave me. . . .
>
> Yours, etc. J. W. Loguen

Frederick Douglass knew that the shame of slavery was not just the South's, that the whole nation was complicit in it. On the Fourth of July, 1852, he gave an Independence Day address:

Fellow Citizens: Pardon me, and allow me to ask, why am I called upon to speak here today? What have I or those I represent to do with your national independence? Are the great principles of political freedom and of natural justice, embodied in that Declaration of Independence, extended to us? And am I, therefore, called upon to bring our humble offering to the national altar, and to confess the benefits, and express devout gratitude for the blessings resulting from your independence to us? . . .

What to the American slave is your Fourth of July? I answer, a day that reveals to him more than all other days of the year, the gross injustice and cruelty to which he is the constant victim. To him your celebration is a sham; your boasted liberty an unholy license; your national greatness, swelling vanity; your sounds of rejoicing are empty and heartless; your denunciation of tyrants, brass-fronted impudence; your shouts of liberty and equality, hollow mockery; your prayers and hymns, your sermons and thanksgivings, with all your religious parade and solemnity, are to him mere bombast, fraud, deception, impiety, and hypocrisy—a thin veil to cover up crimes which would disgrace a nation of savages. There is not a nation of the earth guilty of practices more shocking and bloody than are the people of these United States at this very hour.

Go where you may, search where you will, roam through all the monarchies and despotisms of the Old World, travel through South America, search out every abuse and when you have found the last, lay your facts by the side of the everyday practices of this nation, and you will say with me that, for revolting barbarity and shameless hypocrisy, America reigns without a rival. . . .

Ten years after Nat Turner's rebellion, there was no sign of black insurrection in the South. But that year, 1841, one incident took place which kept alive the idea of rebellion. Slaves being transported on a ship, the *Creole*, overpowered the crew, killed one of them, and sailed into the British West Indies (where slavery had been abolished in 1833). England refused to return the slaves (there was much agitation in England against American slavery), and this led to angry talk in Congress of war with England, encouraged by Secretary of State Daniel Webster. The *Colored Peoples Press* denounced Webster's "bullying position," and, recalling the Revolutionary War and the War of 1812, wrote:

If war be declared . . . Will we fight in defense of a government which denies us the most precious right of citizenship? . . . The States in which we dwell have twice availed themselves of our voluntary services, and have repaid us with chains and slavery. Shall we a third time kiss the foot that crushes us? If so, we deserve our chains.

As the tension grew, North and South, blacks

became more militant. Frederick Douglass spoke in 1857:

> Let me give you a word of the philosophy of re-
> forms. The whole history of the progress of hu-
> man liberty shows that all concessions yet made to
> her august claims have been born of struggle. . . .
> If there is no struggle there is no progress. Those
> who profess to favor freedom and yet deprecate
> agitation, are men who want crops without plow-
> ing up the ground. They want rain without thun-
> der and lightning. They want the ocean without
> the awful roar of its many waters. The struggle
> may be a moral one; or it may be a physical one;
> or it may be both moral and physical, but it must
> be a struggle. Power concedes nothing without a
> demand. It never did and it never will. . . .

There were tactical differences between Douglass and William Lloyd Garrison, white abolitionist and editor of *The Liberator*—differences between
black and white abolitionists in general. Blacks were
more willing to engage in armed insurrection, but
also more ready to use existing political devices—
the ballot box, the Constitution—anything to further their cause. They were not as morally absolute
in their tactics as the Garrisonians. Moral pressure
would not do it alone, the blacks knew; it would take
all sorts of tactics, from elections to rebellion.

How ever-present in the minds of northern Negroes was the question of slavery is shown by black
children in a Cincinnati school, a private school fi-
nanced by Negroes. The children were responding

to the question "What do you think *most* about?" Only five answers remain in the records, and all refer to slavery. A seven-year-old child wrote:

> Dear schoolmates, we are going next summer to buy a farm and to work part of the day and to study the other part if we live to see it and come home part of the day to see our mothers and sisters and cousins if we are got any and see our kind folks and to be good boys and when we get a man to get the poor slaves from bondage. And I am sorrow to hear that the boat . . . went down with 200 poor slaves from up the river. Oh how sorrow I am to hear that, it grieves my heart so that I could faint in one minute.

White abolitionists did courageous and pioneering work, on the lecture platform, in newspapers, in the Underground Railroad. Black abolitionists, less publicized, were the backbone of the antislavery movement. Before Garrison published his famous *Liberator* in Boston in 1831, the first national convention of Negroes had been held, David Walker had already written his "Appeal," and a black abolitionist magazine named *Freedom's Journal* had appeared. Of *The Liberator's* first twenty-five subscribers, most were black.

Blacks had to struggle constantly with the unconscious racism of white abolitionists. They also had to insist on their own independent voice. Douglass wrote for *The Liberator,* but in 1847 started his own newspaper in Rochester, *North Star,* which led to a break with Garrison. In 1854, a conference of

Negroes declared: " . . . it is emphatically our battle; no one else can fight it for us. . . . Our relations to the Anti-Slavery movement must be and are changed. Instead of depending upon it we must lead it."

Certain black women faced the triple hurdle—of being abolitionists in a slave society, of being black among white reformers, and of being women in a reform movement dominated by men. When Sojourner Truth rose to speak in 1853 in New York City at the Fourth National Woman's Rights Convention, it all came together. There was a hostile mob in the hall shouting, jeering, threatening. She said:

> I know that it feels a kind o' hissin' and ticklin' like to see a colored woman get up and tell you about things, and Woman's Rights. We have all been thrown down so low that nobody thought we'd ever get up again; but . . . we will come up again, and now I'm here. . . . we'll have our rights; see if we don't; and you can't stop us from them; see if you can. You may hiss as much as you like, but it is comin'. . . . I am sittin' among you to watch; and every once and awhile I will come out and tell you what time of night it is. . . .

After Nat Turner's violent uprising and Virginia's bloody repression, the security system inside the South became tighter. Perhaps only an outsider could hope to launch a rebellion. It was such a person, a white man of ferocious courage and determination, John Brown, whose wild scheme it was to seize the federal arsenal at Harpers Ferry, Virginia, and then set off a revolt of slaves through the South.

Harriet Tubman, 5 feet tall, some of her teeth missing, a veteran of countless secret missions piloting blacks out of slavery, was involved with John Brown and his plans. But sickness prevented her from joining him. Frederick Douglass too had met with Brown, He argued against the plan from the standpoint of its chances of success, but he admired the ailing man of sixty, tall, gaunt, white-haired.

Douglass was right; the plan would not work. The local militia, joined by a hundred marines under the command of Robert E. Lee, surrounded the insurgents. Although his men were dead or captured, John Brown refused to surrender: he barricaded himself in a small brick building near the gate of the armory. The troops battered down a door; a marine lieutenant moved in and struck Brown with his sword. Wounded, sick, he was interrogated. W.E.B. DuBois, in his book *John Brown,* writes:

> Picture the situation: An old and blood-bespattered man, half-dead from the wounds inflicted but a few hours before; a man lying in the cold and dirt, without sleep for fifty-five nerve-wrecking hours, without food for nearly as long, with the dead bodies of his two sons almost before his eyes, the piled corpses of his seven slain comrades near and afar, a wife and a bereaved family listening in vain, and a Lost Cause, the dream of a lifetime, lying dead in his heart. . . .

Lying there, interrogated by the governor of Virginia, Brown said: "You had betters—all you people at the South—prepare yourselves for a settlement of

this question. . . . You may dispose of me very easily—
I am nearly disposed of now, but this question is still
to be settled,—this Negro question, I mean; the end
of that is not yet."

Du Bois appraises Brown's action:

> If his foray was the work of a handful of fanatics,
> led by a lunatic and repudiated by the slaves to a
> man, then the proper procedure would have been
> to ignore the incident, quietly punish the worst of-
> fenders and either pardon the misguided leader
> or send him to an asylum. . . . While insisting that
> the raid was too hopelessly and ridiculously small
> to accomplish anything . . . the state nevertheless
> spent $250,000 to punish the invaders, stationed
> from one to three thousand soldiers in the vicinity
> and threw the nation into turmoil.

In John Brown's last written statement, in prison,
before he was hanged, he said: "I, John Brown, am
quite certain that the crimes of this guilty land will
never be purged away but with blood."

Ralph Waldo Emerson, not an activist himself,
said of the execution of John Brown: "He will make
the gallows holy as the cross."

Of the twenty-two men in John Brown's striking
force, five were black. Two of these were killed on
the spot, one escaped, and two were hanged by the
authorities. Before his execution, John Copeland
wrote to his parents:

> Remember that if I must die I die in trying to lib-
> erate a few of my poor and oppressed people from

my condition of servitude which God in his Holy Writ has hurled his most bitter denunciations against. . . .

I am not terrified by the gallows. . . .

I imagine that I hear you, and all of you, mother, father, sisters, and brothers, say—"No, there is not a cause for which we, with less sorrow, could see you die." Believe me when I tell you, that though shut up in prison and under sentence of death, I have spent more happy hours here, and . . . I would almost as lief die now as at any time, for I feel that I am prepared to meet my Maker. . . .

John Brown was executed by the state of Virginia with the approval of the national government. It was the national government which, while weakly enforcing the law ending the slave trade, sternly enforced the laws providing for the return of fugitives to slavery. It was the national government that, in Andrew Jackson's administration, collaborated with the South to keep abolitionist literature out of the mails in the southern states. It was the Supreme Court of the United States that declared in 1857 that the slave Dred Scott could not sue for his freedom because he was not a person, but property.

Such a national government would never accept an end to slavery by rebellion. It would end slavery only under conditions controlled by whites, and only when required by the political and economic needs of the business elite of the North. It was Abraham Lincoln who combined perfectly the needs of business, the political ambition of the new Republican

party, and the rhetoric of humanitarianism. He
would keep the abolition of slavery not at the top of
his list of priorities, but close enough to the top so
it could be pushed there temporarily by abolitionist
pressures and by practical political advantage.

Lincoln could skillfully blend the interests of the
very rich and the interests of the black at a moment
in history when these interests met. And he could link
these two with a growing section of Americans, the
white, up-and-coming, economically ambitious, politically active middle class. As Richard Hofstadter puts it:

> Thoroughly middle class in his ideas, he spoke for
> those millions of Americans who had begun their
> lives as hired workers—as farm hands, clerks, teach-
> ers, mechanics, flatboat men, and rail-splitters—and
> had passed into the ranks of landed farmers, pros-
> perous grocers, lawyers, merchants, physicians and
> politicians.

Lincoln could argue with lucidity and passion
against slavery on moral grounds, while acting cau-
tiously in practical politics. He believed "that the institution of slavery is founded on injustice and bad
policy, but that the promulgation of abolition doc-
trines tends to increase rather than abate its evils."
(Put against this Frederick Douglass's statement on
struggle, or Garrison's "Sir, slavery will not be over-
thrown without excitement, a most tremendous excitement.") Lincoln read the Constitution strictly, to
mean that Congress, because of the Tenth Amendment (reserving to the states powers not specifically
given to the national government), could not consti-

tutionally bar slavery in the states.

When it was proposed to abolish slavery in the District of Columbia, which did not have the rights of a state but was directly under the jurisdiction of Congress, Lincoln said this would be Constitutional, but it should not be done unless the people in the District wanted it. Since most there were white, this killed the idea. As Hofstadter said of Lincoln's statement, it "breathes the fire of an uncompromising insistence on moderation."

Lincoln refused to denounce the Fugitive Slave Law publicly. He wrote to a friend: "I confess I hate to see the poor creatures hunted down . . . but I bite my lips and keep quiet." And when he did propose, in 1849, as a Congressman, a resolution to abolish slavery in the District of Columbia, he accompanied this with a section requiring local authorities to arrest and return fugitive slaves coming into Washington. (This led Wendell Phillips, the Boston abolitionist, to refer to him years later as "that slavehound from Illinois.") He opposed slavery, but could not see blacks as equals, so a constant theme in his approach was to free the slaves and to send them back to Africa.

In his 1858 campaign in Illinois for the Senate against Stephen Douglas, Lincoln spoke differently depending on the views of his listeners (and also perhaps depending on how close it was to the election). Speaking in northern Illinois in July (in Chicago), he said:

> Let us discard all this quibbling about this man and the other man, this race and that race and the other race being inferior, and therefore they must

be placed in an inferior position. Let us discard all
these things, and unite as one people throughout
this land, until we shall once more stand up declaring that all men are created equal.

Two months later in Charleston, in southern Illinois, Lincoln told his audience:

I will say, then, that I am not, nor ever have been,
in favor of bringing about in any way the social
and political equality of the white and black races
(applause); that I am not, nor ever have been, in
favor of making voters or jurors of negroes, nor of
qualifying them to hold office, nor to intermarry
with white people. . . .
   And inasmuch as they cannot so live, while
they do remain together there must be the position of superior and inferior, and I as much as any
other man am in favor of having the superior position assigned to the white race.

Behind the secession of the South from the
Union, after Lincoln was elected President in the
fall of 1860 as candidate of the new Republican
party, was a long series of policy clashes between
South and North. The clash was not over slavery as
a moral institution—most northerners did not care
enough about slavery to make sacrifices for it, certainly not the sacrifice of war. It was not a clash of
peoples (most northern whites were not economically favored, not politically powerful; most southern whites were poor farmers, not decisionmakers)
but of elites. The northern elite wanted economic

expansion—free land, free labor, a free market, a high protective tariff for manufacturers, a bank of the United States. The slave interests opposed all that; they saw Lincoln and the Republicans as making continuation of their pleasant and prosperous way of life impossible in the future.

So, when Lincoln was elected, seven southern states seceded from the Union. Lincoln initiated hostilities by trying to repossess the federal base at Fort Sumter, South Carolina, and four more states seceded. The Confederacy was formed; the Civil War was on.

Lincoln's first Inaugural Address, in March 1861, was conciliatory toward the South and the seceded states: "I have no purpose, directly or indirectly, to interfere with the institution of slavery in the States where it exists. I believe I have no lawful right to do so, and I have no inclination to do so." And with the war four months on, when General John C. Frémont in Missouri declared martial law and said slaves of owners resisting the United States were to be free, Lincoln countermanded this order. He was anxious to hold in the Union the slave states of Maryland, Kentucky, Missouri, and Delaware.

It was only as the war grew more bitter, the casualties mounted, desperation to win heightened, and the criticism of the abolitionists threatened to unravel the tattered coalition behind Lincoln that he began to act against slavery. Hofstadter puts it this way: "Like a delicate barometer, he recorded the trend of pressures, and as the Radical pressure increased he moved toward the left." Wendell Phillips said that if Lincoln was able to grow "it is because we have watered him."

Racism in the North was as entrenched as slavery in the South, and it would take the war to shake both. New York blacks could not vote unless they owned $250 in property (a qualification not applied to whites). A proposal to abolish this, put on the ballot in 1860, was defeated two to one (although Lincoln carried New York by 50,000 votes). Frederick Douglass commented: "The black baby of Negro suffrage was thought too ugly to exhibit on so grand an occasion. The Negro was stowed away like some people put out of sight their deformed children when company comes."

Wendell Phillips, with all his criticism of Lincoln, recognized the possibilities in his election. Speaking at the Tremont Temple in Boston the day after the election, Phillips said:

> If the telegraph speaks truth, for the first time in our history the slave has chosen a President of the United States. . . . Not an Abolitionist, hardly an antislavery man, Mr. Lincoln consents to represent an antislavery idea. A pawn on the political chessboard, his value is in his position; with fair effort, we may soon change him for knight, bishop or queen, and sweep the board. (Applause)

Conservatives in the Boston upper classes wanted reconciliation with the South. At one point they stormed an abolitionist meeting at that same Tremont Temple, shortly after Lincoln's election, and asked that concessions be made to the South "in the interests of commerce, manufactures, agriculture."

The spirit of Congress, even after the war began, was shown in a resolution it passed in the summer of 1861, with only a few dissenting votes: " . . . this war is not waged . . . for any purpose of . . . overthrowing or interfering with the rights of established institutions of those states, but . . . to preserve the Union."

The abolitionists stepped up their campaign. Emancipation petitions poured into Congress in 1861 and 1862. In May of that year, Wendell Phillips said: "Abraham Lincoln may not wish it; he cannot prevent it; the nation may not will it, but the nation cannot prevent it. I do not care what men want or wish; the negro is the pebble in the cog-wheel, and the machine cannot go on until you get him out."

In July Congress passed a Confiscation Act, which enabled the freeing of slaves of those fighting the Union. But this was not enforced by the Union generals, and Lincoln ignored the nonenforcement. Garrison called Lincoln's policy "stumbling, halting, prevaricating, irresolute, weak, besotted," and Phillips said Lincoln was "a first-rate second-rate man."

An exchange of letters between Lincoln and Horace Greeley, editor of the New York *Tribune*, in August of 1862, gave Lincoln a chance to express his views. Greeley wrote:

> Dear Sir. I do not intrude to tell you—for you must know already—that a great proportion of those who triumphed in your election . . . are sorely disappointed and deeply pained by the policy you seem to be pursuing with regard to the slaves of rebels. . . . We require of you, as the first servant of the Republic, charged especially and

preeminently with this duty, that you EXECUTE
THE LAWS. . . . We think you are strangely and
disastrously remiss . . . with regard to the emancipating provisions of the new Confiscation Act. . . .

We think you are unduly influenced by the
councils . . . of certain politicians hailing from the
Border Slave States.

Greeley appealed to the practical need of winning the war. "We must have scouts, guides, spies,
cooks, teamsters, diggers and choppers from the
blacks of the South, whether we allow them to fight
for us or not. . . . I entreat you to render a hearty and
unequivocal obedience to the law of the land."

Lincoln had already shown his attitude by his
failure to countermand an order of one of his com-
manders, General Henry Halleck, who forbade fugitive Negroes to enter his army's lines. Now he re-
plied to Greeley:

Dear Sir: . . . I have not meant to leave any one in
doubt. . . . My paramount object in this struggle
is to save the Union, and is not either to save or
destroy Slavery. If I could save the Union without freeing any slave, I would do it; and if I could
save it by freeing all the slaves, I would do it; and
if I could do it by freeing some and leaving others alone, I would also do that. What I do about
Slavery and the colored race, I do because it helps
to save this Union; and what I forbear, I forbear
because I do not believe it would help to save the
Union. . . . I have here stated my purpose according to my view of official duty, and I intend no

modification of my oft-expressed personal wish
that all men, everywhere, could be free. Yours. A.
Lincoln.

So Lincoln distinguished between his "personal
wish" and his "official duty."

When in September 1862, Lincoln issued his
preliminary Emancipation Proclamation, it was a
military move, giving the South four months to stop
rebelling, threatening to emancipate their slaves if
they continued to fight, promising to leave slavery
untouched in states that came over to the North:

> That on the 1st day of January, AD 1863, all per-
> sons held as slaves within any State or designated
> part of a State the people whereof shall then be in
> rebellion against the United States shall be then,
> thenceforward and forever free. . . .

Thus, when the Emancipation Proclamation was
issued January 1, 1863, it declared slaves free in those
areas still fighting against the Union (which it listed
very carefully), and said nothing about slaves behind
Union lines. As Hofstadter put it, the Emancipation
Proclamation "had all the moral grandeur of a bill of
lading." The *London Spectator* wrote concisely: "The
principle is not that a human being cannot justly own
another, but that he cannot own him unless he is loyal
to the United States."

Limited as it was, the Emancipation Proclamation spurred antislavery forces. By the summer of
1864, 400,000 signatures asking legislation to end
slavery had been gathered and sent to Congress,

something unprecedented in the history of the country. That April, the Senate had adopted the Thirteenth Amendment, declaring an end to slavery, and in January 1865, the House of Representatives followed.

With the Proclamation, the Union army was open to blacks. And the more blacks entered the war, the more it appeared a war for their liberation. The more whites had to sacrifice, the more resentment there was, particularly among poor whites in the North, who were drafted by a law that allowed the rich to buy their way out of the draft for $300. And so the draft riots of 1863 took place, uprisings of angry whites in northern cities, their targets not the rich, far away, but the blacks, near at hand. It was an orgy of death and violence. A black man in Detroit described what he saw: a mob, with kegs of beer on wagons, armed with clubs and bricks, marching through the city, attacking black men, women, children. He heard one man say: "If we are got to be killed up for Negroes then we will kill every one in this town."

The Civil War was one of the bloodiest in human history up to that time: 600,000 dead on both sides, in a population of 30 million—the equivalent, in the United States of 1978, with a population of 250 million, of 5 million dead. As the battles became more intense, as the bodies piled up, as war fatigue grew, the existence of blacks in the South, 4 million of them, became more and more a hindrance to the South, and more and more an opportunity for the North. Du Bois, in *Black Reconstruction*, pointed this out:

. . . these slaves had enormous power in their
hands. Simply by stopping work, they could
threaten the Confederacy with starvation. By
walking into the Federal camps, they showed to
doubting Northerners the easy possibility of using them thus, but by the same gesture, depriving
their enemies of their use in just these fields. . . .

It was this plain alternative that brought Lee's
sudden surrender. Either the South must make
terms with its slaves, free them, use them to fight
the North, and thereafter no longer treat them as
bondsmen; or they could surrender to the North
with the assumption that the North after the war
must help them to defend slavery, as it had before.

George Rawick, a sociologist and anthropologist,
describes the development of blacks up to and into
the Civil War:

The slaves went from being frightened human be-
ings, thrown among strange men, including fellow slaves who were not their kinsmen and who
did not speak their language or understand their
customs and habits, to what W.E.B. DuBois once
described as the general strike whereby hundreds
of thousands of slaves deserted the plantations,
destroying the South's ability to supply its army.

Black women played an important part in the
war, especially toward the end. Sojourner Truth,
the legendary ex-slave who had been active in the
women's rights movement, became recruiter of
black troops for the Union army, as did Josephine

St. Pierre Ruffin of Boston. Harriet Tubman raided plantations, leading black and white troops, and
in one expedition freed 750 slaves. Women moved
with the colored regiments that grew as the Union
army marched through the South, helping their
husbands, enduring terrible hardships on the long
military treks, in which many children died. They
suffered the fate of soldiers, as in April 1864, when
Confederate troops at Fort Pillow, Kentucky, massacred Union soldiers who had surrendered—black
and white, along with women and children in an ad-
joining camp.

It has been said that black acceptance of slavery
is proved by the fact that during the Civil War, when
there were opportunities for escape, most slaves
stayed on the plantation. In fact, half a million ran
away—about one in five, a high proportion when one
considers that there was great difficulty in knowing
where to go and how to live.

The owner of a large plantation in South Carolina and Georgia wrote in 1862: "This war has taught
us the perfect impossibility of placing the least confidence in the negro. In too numerous instances those
we esteemed the most have been the first to desert
us." That same year, a lieutenant in the Confederate
army and once mayor of Savannah, Georgia, wrote:
"I deeply regret to learn that the Negroes still continue to desert to the enemy."

A minister in Mississippi wrote in the fall of 1862:
"On my arrival was surprised to hear that our negroes stampeded to the Yankees last night or rather
a portion of them. . . . I think every one, but with
one or two exceptions will go to the Yankees. Eliza

and her family are certain to go. She does not conceal her thoughts but plainly manifests her opinions by her conduct—insolent and insulting." And a woman's plantation journal of January 1865:

> The people are all idle on the plantations, most of them seeking their own pleasure. Many servants have proven faithful, others false and rebellious against all authority and restraint. . . . Their condition is one of perfect anarchy and rebellion. They have placed themselves in perfect antagonism to their owners and to all government and control. . . . Nearly all the house servants have left their homes; and from most of the plantations they have gone in a body.

Also in 1865, a South Carolina planter wrote to the New York *Tribune* that

> the conduct of the Negro in the late crisis of our affairs has convinced me that we were all laboring under a delusion. . . . I believed that these people were content, happy, and attached to their masters. But events and reflection have caused me to change these positions. . . . If they were content, happy and attached to their masters, why did they desert him in the moment of his need and flock to an enemy, whom they did not know; and thus left their perhaps really good masters whom they did know from infancy?

Genovese notes that the war produced no general rising of slaves, but: "In Lafayette County,

Mississippi, slaves responded to the Emancipation Proclamation by driving off their overseers and dividing the land and implements among themselves." Aptheker reports a conspiracy of Negroes in Arkansas in 1861 to kill their enslavers. In Kentucky that year, houses and barns were burned by Negroes, and in the city of New Castle slaves paraded through the city "singing political songs, and shouting for Lincoln," according to newspaper accounts. After the Emancipation Proclamation, a Negro waiter in Richmond, Virginia, was arrested for leading "a servile plot," while in Yazoo City, Mississippi, slaves burned the courthouse and fourteen homes.

There were special moments: Robert Smalls (later a South Carolina Congressman) and other blacks took over a steamship, *The Planter,* and sailed it past the Confederate guns to deliver it to the Union navy.

Most slaves neither submitted nor rebelled. They continued to work, waiting to see what happened. When opportunity came, they left, often joining the Union army. Two hundred thousand blacks were in the army and navy, and 38,000 were killed. Historian James McPherson says: "Without their help, the North could not have won the war as soon as it did, and perhaps it could not have won at all."

What happened to blacks in the Union army and in the northern cities during the war gave some hint of how limited the emancipation would be, even with full victory over the Con-

THE OTHER CIVIL WAR   41

federacy. Off-duty black soldiers were attacked in
northern cities, as in Zanesville, Ohio, in February
1864, where cries were heard to "kill the nigger."
Black soldiers were used for the heaviest and dirtiest
work, digging trenches, hauling logs and cannon,
loading ammunition, digging wells for white regiments. White privates received $13 a month; Negro
privates received $10 a month.

Late in the war, a black sergeant of the Third
South Carolina Volunteers, William Walker,
marched his company to his captain's tent and ordered them to stack arms and resign from the army
as a protest against what he considered a breach
of contract, because of unequal pay. He was court-
martialed and shot for mutiny. Finally, in June 1864,
Congress passed a law granting equal pay to Negro
soldiers.

The Confederacy was desperate in the latter part
of the war, and some of its leaders suggested the
slaves, more and more an obstacle to their cause, be
enlisted, used, and freed. After a number of military
defeats, the Confederate secretary of war, Judah
Benjamin, wrote in late 1864 to a newspaper editor
in Charleston: " . . . It is well known that General
Lee, who commands so largely the confidence of the
people, is strongly in favor of our using the negroes
for defense, and emancipating them, if necessary, for
that purpose. . . ." One general, indignant, wrote: "If
slaves will make good soldiers, our whole theory of
slavery is wrong."

By early 1865, the pressure had mounted, and in
March President Davis of the Confederacy signed a
"Negro Soldier Law" authorizing the enlistment of

slaves as soldiers, to be freed by consent of their owners and their state governments. But before it had
any significant effect, the war was over.

Former slaves, interviewed by the Federal Writers' Project in the thirties, recalled the war's end.
Susie Melton:

> I was a young gal, about ten years old, and we
> done heard that Lincoln gonna turn the nig-
> gers free. Ol' missus say there wasn't nothin' to
> it. Then a Yankee soldier told someone in Wil-
> liamsburg that Lincoln done signed the 'mancipa-
> tion. Was wintertime and mighty cold that night,
> but everybody commenced getting ready to leave.
> Didn't care nothin' about missus—was going to
> the Union lines. And all that night the niggers
> danced and sang right out in the cold. Next morn-
> ing at day break we all started out with blankets
> and clothes and pots and pans and chickens piled
> on our backs, 'cause missus said we couldn't take
> no horses or carts. And as the sun come up over
> the trees, the niggers started to singing:
>
> *Sun, you be here and I'll be gone*
> *Sun, you be here and I'll be gone*
> *Sun, you be here and I'll be gone*
> *Bye, bye, don't grieve after me*
> *Won't give you my place, not for yours*
> *Bye, bye, don't grieve after me*
> *Cause you be here and I'll be gone.*

Anna Woods:

We wasn't there in Texas long when the soldiers marched in to tell us that we were free. . . . I remembers one woman. She jumped on a barrel and she shouted. She jumped off and she shouted. She jumped back on again and shouted some more. She kept that up for a long time, just jumping on a barrel and back off again.

Annie Mae Weathers said:

I remember hearing my pa say that when somebody came and hollered, "You niggers is free at last," say he just dropped his hoe and said in a queer voice, "Thank God for that."

The Federal Writers' Project recorded an ex-slave named Fannie Berry:

Niggers shoutin' and clappin' hands and singin'! Chillun runnin' all over the place beatin' time and yellin'! Everybody happy. Sho' did some celebratin'.
    Run to the kitchen and shout in the window:
    "Mammy, don't you cook no more.
    You's free! You's free!"

Many Negroes understood that their status after the war, whatever their situation legally, would depend on whether they owned the land they worked on or would be forced to be semislaves for others. In 1863, a North Carolina Negro wrote that "if the strict law of right and justice is to be observed, the country around me is the entailed inheritance of the Americans of African descent, purchased by the invaluable labor of our ancestors, through a life of tears and groans, under the lash and yoke of tyranny."

Abandoned plantations, however, were leased to former planters, and to white men of the North. As one colored newspaper said: "The slaves were made serfs and chained to the soil. . . . Such was the boasted freedom acquired by the colored man at the hands of the Yankee."

Under congressional policy approved by Lincoln, the property confiscated during the war under the Confiscation Act of July 1862 would revert to the heirs of the Confederate owners. Dr. John Rock, a black physician in Boston, spoke at a meeting: "Why talk about compensating masters? Compensate them for what? What do you owe them? What does the slave owe them? What does society owe them? Compensate the master? . . . It is the slave who ought to be compensated. The property of the South is by right the property of the slave. . . ."

Some land was expropriated on grounds the taxes were delinquent, and sold at auction. But only a few blacks could afford to buy this. In the South Carolina Sea Islands, out of 16,000 acres up for sale in March of 1863, freedmen who pooled their money were able to buy 2,000 acres, the rest being bought by northern investors and speculators. A freedman on the Islands dictated a letter to a former teacher now in Philadelphia:

My Dear Young Missus: Do, my missus, tell Linkum dat we wants land—dis bery land dat is rich

wid de sweat ob de face and de blood ob we back.
. . . We could a bin buy all we want, but dey make
de lots too big, and cut we out.

De word cum from Mass Linkum's self, dat we
take out claims and hold on ter um, an' plant um,
and he will see dat we get um, every man ten or
twenty acre. We too glad. We stake out an' list, but
fore de time for plant, dese commissionaries sells
to white folks all de best land. Where Linkum?

In early 1865, General William T. Sherman
held a conference in Savannah, Georgia, with twenty
Negro ministers and church officials, mostly former slaves, at which one of them expressed their
need: "The way we can best take care of ourselves is
to have land, and till it by our labor. . . ." Four days
later Sherman issued "Special Field Order No. 15,"
designating the entire southern coastline 30 miles
inland for exclusive Negro settlement. Freedmen
could settle there, taking no more than 40 acres
per family. By June 1865, forty thousand freedmen
had moved onto new farms in this area. But President Andrew Johnson, in August of 1865, restored
this land to the Confederate owners, and the freedmen were forced off, some at bayonet point.

Ex-slave Thomas Hall told the Federal Writers'
Project:

Lincoln got the praise for freeing us, but did he
do it? He gave us freedom without giving us any
chance to live to ourselve and we still had to depend on the southern white man for work, food,
and clothing, and he held us out of necessity and

want in a state of servitude but little better than slavery.

The American government had set out to fight the slave states in 1861, not to end slavery, but to retain the enormous national territory and market and resources. Yet, victory required a crusade, and the momentum of that crusade brought new forces into national politics: more blacks determined to make their freedom mean something; more whites—whether Freedman's Bureau officials, or teachers in the Sea Islands, or "carpetbaggers" with various mixtures of humanitarianism and personal ambition—concerned with racial equality. There was also the powerful interest of the Republican party in maintaining control over the national government, with the prospect of southern black votes to accomplish this. Northern businessmen, seeing Republican policies as beneficial to them, went along for a while.

The result was that brief period after the Civil War in which southern Negroes voted, elected blacks to state legislatures and to Congress, introduced free and racially mixed public education to the South. A legal framework was constructed. The Thirteenth Amendment outlawed slavery: "Neither slavery nor involuntary servitude, except as a punishment for crime whereof the party shall have been duly convicted, shall exist within the United States, or any place subject to their jurisdiction." The Fourteenth Amendment repudiated the prewar Dred Scott decision by declaring that "all persons born or naturalized in the United States" were citizens. It also seemed to make a powerful statement for racial equality, severely limiting "states' rights":

> No State shall make or enforce any law which shall abridge the privileges or immunities of citizens of the United States; nor shall any State deprive any person of life, liberty, or property, without due process of law; nor deny to any person within its jurisdiction the equal protection of the laws.

The Fifteenth Amendment said: "The right of citizens of the United States to vote shall not be denied or abridged by the United States or by any State on account of race, color, or previous condition of servitude."

Congress passed a number of laws in the late 1860s and early 1870s in the same spirit—laws making it a crime to deprive Negroes of their rights, requiring federal officials to enforce those rights, giving Negroes the right to enter contracts and buy property without discrimination. And in 1875, a Civil Rights Act outlawed the exclusion of Negroes from hotels, theaters, railroads, and other public accommodations.

With these laws, with the Union army in the South as protection, and a civilian army of officials in the Freedman's Bureau to help them, southern Negroes came forward, voted, formed political organizations, and expressed themselves forcefully on issues important to them. They were hampered in this for several years by Andrew Johnson, Vice-President under Lincoln, who became President when Lincoln was assassinated at the close of the war. Johnson vetoed bills to help Negroes; he made it easy for Confederate states to come back into the Union without guaranteeing equal rights to blacks. During his presidency, these returned southern states enacted "black codes," which made the freed slaves like serfs, still working the plantations. For instance, Mississippi in 1865 made it illegal for freedmen to rent or lease farmland, and provided for them to work under labor contracts which they could not break under penalty of prison. It also provided that the courts could assign black children under eighteen who had no parents, or whose parents were poor, to forced labor, called apprenticeships—with punishment for runaways.

Andrew Johnson clashed with Senators and Congressmen who, in some cases for reasons of justice, in others out of political calculation, supported equal rights and voting for the freedman. These members of Congress succeeded in impeaching Johnson in 1868, using as an excuse that he had violated some minor statute, but the Senate fell one vote short of the two-thirds required to remove him from office. In the presidential election of that year, Republican Ulysses Grant was elected, winning by 300,000 votes, with 700,000 Negroes voting, and so Johnson was out as an obstacle. Now the southern states could come back into the Union only by approving the new Constitutional amendments.

Whatever northern politicians were doing to help their cause, southern blacks were determined to make the most of their freedom, in spite of their lack of land and resources. A study of blacks in Alabama in the first years after the war by historian Peter Kolchin finds that they began immediately asserting their independence of whites, forming their own churches, becoming politically active, strengthening their family ties, trying to educate their children. Kolchin disagrees with the contention of some historians that slavery had created a "Sambo" mentality of submission among blacks. "As soon as they were free, these supposedly dependent, childlike Negroes began acting like independent men and women."

Negroes were now elected to southern state legislatures, although in all these they were a minority except in the lower house of the South Carolina legislature. A great propaganda campaign was undertaken in the North and South (one which lasted well into the twentieth century, in the history textbooks of American schools) to show that blacks were inept, lazy, corrupt, and ruinous to the governments of the South when they were in office. Undoubtedly there was corruption, but one could hardly claim that blacks had invented political conniving, especially in the bizarre climate of financial finagling North and South after the Civil War.

It was true that the public debt of South Carolina, $7 million in 1865, went up to $29 million in 1873, but the new legislature introduced free public schools for the first time into the state. Not only were seventy thousand Negro children going to school by 1876 where none had gone before, but fifty thousand white children were going to school where only twenty thousand had attended in 1860.

Black voting in the period after 1869 resulted in two Negro members of the U.S. Senate (Hiram Revels and Blanche Bruce, both from Mississippi), and twenty Congressmen, including eight from South

Carolina, four from North Carolina, three from Alabama, and one each from the other former Confederate states. (This list would dwindle rapidly after
1876; the last black left Congress in 1901.)

A Columbia University scholar of the twentieth
century, John Burgess, referred to Black Reconstruction as follows:

> In place of government by the most intelligent
> and virtuous part of the people for the benefit of
> the governed, here was government by the most
> ignorant and vicious part of the population. . . .
> A black skin means membership in a race of men
> which has never of itself succeeded in subjecting
> passion to reason; has never, therefore, created
> civilization of any kind.

One has to measure against those words the black
leaders in the postwar South. For instance, Henry
MacNeal Turner, who had escaped from peonage
on a South Carolina plantation at the age of fifteen,
taught himself to read and write, read law books
while a messenger in a lawyer's office in Baltimore,
and medical books while a handyman in a Baltimore
medical school, served as chaplain to a Negro regiment, and then was elected to the first postwar legislature of Georgia. In 1868, the Georgia legislature
voted to expel all its Negro members—two senators, twenty-five representatives—and Turner spoke
to the Georgia House of Representatives (a black
woman graduate student at Atlanta University later
brought his speech to light):

Mr. Speaker. . . . I wish the members of this House to understand the position that I take. I hold that I am a member of this body. Therefore, sir, I shall neither fawn or cringe before any party, nor stoop to beg them for my rights. . . . I am here to demand my rights, and to hurl thunderbolts at the men who would dare to cross the threshold of my manhood. . . .

The scene presented in this House, today, is one unparalleled in the history of the world. . . . Never, in the history of the world, has a man been arraigned before a body clothed with legislative, judicial or executive functions, charged with the offense of being of a darker hue than his fellow-men. . . . it has remained for the State of Georgia, in the very heart of the nineteenth century, to call a man before the bar, and there charge him with an act for which he is no more responsible than for the head which he carries upon his shoulders. The Anglo-Saxon race, sir, is a most surprising one. . . . I was not aware that there was in the character of that race so much cowardice, or so much pusillanimity. . . . I tell you, sir, that this is a question which will not die today. This event shall be remembered by posterity for ages yet to come, and while the sun shall continue to climb the hills of heaven. . . .

. . . we are told that if black men want to speak, they must speak through white trumpets; if black men want their sentiments expressed, they must be adulterated and sent through white messengers, who will quibble, and equivocate, and evade, as rapidly as the pendulum of a clock. . . .

The great question, sir is this: Am I a man? If I am such, I claim the rights of a man. . . .

Why, sir, though we are not white, we have accomplished much. We have pioneered civilization here; we have built up your country; we have worked in your fields, and garnered your harvests, for two hundred and fifty years! And what do we ask of you in return? Do we ask you for compensation for the sweat our fathers bore for you—for the tears you have caused, and the hearts you have broken, and the lives you have curtailed, and the blood you have spilled? Do we ask retaliation? We ask it not. We are willing to let the dead past bury its dead; but we ask you now for our RIGHTS. . . .

As black children went to school, they were encouraged by teachers, black and white, to express themselves freely, sometimes in catechism style. The records of a school in Louisville, Kentucky:

Teacher:	Now children, you don't think white people are any better than you because they have straight hair and white faces?
Students:	No, sir.
Teacher:	No, they are no better, but they are different, they possess great power, they formed this great government, they control this vast country. . . . Now what makes them different from you?
Students:	Money!
Teacher:	Yes, but what enabled them to obtain it? How did they get money?
Students:	Got it off us, stole it off we all!

Black women helped rebuild the postwar South. Frances Ellen Watkins Harper, born free in Baltimore, self-supporting from the age of thirteen, working as a nursemaid, later as an abolitionist lecturer, reader of her own poetry, spoke all through the southern states after the war. She was a feminist, participant in the 1866 Woman's Rights Convention, and founder of the National Association of Colored Women. In the 1890s she wrote the first novel published by a black woman: *Iola Leroy or Shadows Uplifted*. In 1878 she described what she had seen and heard recently in the South:

> An acquaintance of mine, who lives in South Carolina, and has been engaged in mission work, reports that, in supporting the family, women are the mainstay; that two-thirds of the truck gardening is done by them in South Carolina; that in the city they are more industrious than the men. . . . When the men lose their work through their political affiliations, the women stand by them, and say, "stand by your principles."

Through all the struggles to gain equal rights for blacks, certain black women spoke out on their special situation. Sojourner Truth, at a meeting of the American Equal Rights Association, said:

> There is a great stir about colored men getting their rights, but not a word about the colored women; and if colored men get their rights, and not colored women theirs, you see the colored men will be masters over the women, and it will

be just as bad as it was before. So I am for keeping
the thing going while things are stirring; because
if we wait till it is still, it will take a great while to
get it going again. . . .

I am above eighty years old; it is about time
for me to be going. I have been forty years a slave
and forty years free, and would be here forty years
more to have equal rights for all. I suppose I am
kept here because something remains for me to
do; I suppose I am yet to help break the chain. I
have done a great deal of work; as much as a man,
but did not get so much pay. I used to work in the
field and bind grain, keeping with the cradler; but
men doing no more, got twice as much pay. . . . I
suppose I am about the only colored woman that
goes about to speak for the rights of the colored
women. I want to keep the thing stirring, now that
the ice is cracked. . . .

The Constitutional amendments were passed, the
laws for racial equality were passed, and the black man
began to vote and to hold office. But so long as the
Negro remained dependent on privileged whites for
work, for the necessities of life, his vote could be bought
or taken away by threat of force. Thus, laws calling for
equal treatment became meaningless. While Union
troops—including colored troops—remained in the
South, this process was delayed. But the balance of
military powers began to change.

The southern white oligarchy used its economic
power to organize the Ku Klux Klan and other ter-
rorist groups. Northern politicians began to weigh
the advantage of the political support of impover-

ished blacks—maintained in voting and office only by force—against the more stable situation of a South returned to white supremacy, accepting Republican dominance and business legislation. It was only a matter of time before blacks would be reduced once again to conditions not far from slavery.

Violence began almost immediately with the end of the war. In Memphis, Tennessee, in May of 1866, whites on a rampage of murder killed forty-six Negroes, most of them veterans of the Union army, as well as two white sympathizers. Five Negro women were raped. Ninety homes, twelve schools, and four churches were burned. In New Orleans, in the summer of 1866, another riot against blacks killed thirty-five Negroes and three whites.

Mrs. Sarah Song testified before a congressional investigating committee:

Have you been a slave?

I have been a slave.

What did you see of the rioting?

I saw them kill my husband; it was on Tuesday night, between ten and eleven o'clock; he was shot in the head while he was in bed sick. . . . There were between twenty and thirty men. . . . They came into the room. . . . Then one stepped back and shot him. . . . he was not a yard from him; he put the pistol to his head and shot him three times. . . . Then one of them kicked him, and another shot him again when he was down. . . . He never spoke after he fell. They then went running right off and did not come back again. . . .

The violence mounted through the late 1860s
and early 1870s as the Ku Klux Klan organized
raids, lynchings, beatings, burnings. For Kentucky
alone, between 1867 and 1871, the National Archives
lists 116 acts of violence. A sampling:

1.   A mob visited Harrodsburg in Mercer County
      to take from jail a man named Robertson
      Nov. 14, 1867. . . .
5.   Sam Davis hung by a mob in Harrodsburg,
      May 28, 1868.
6.   Wm. Pierce hung by a mob in Christian
      July 12, 1868.
7.   Geo. Roger hung by a mob in Bradsfordville
      Martin County July 11, 1868. . . .
10.   Silas Woodford age sixty badly beaten by
      disguised mob. . . .
109. Negro killed by Ku Klux Klan in Hay
      county January 14, 1871.

A Negro blacksmith named Charles Caldwell,
born a slave, later elected to the Mississippi Senate,
and known as "a notorious and turbulent Negro"
by whites, was shot at by the son of a white Mississippi judge in 1868. Caldwell fired back and killed
the man. Tried by an all-white jury, he argued self-
defense and was acquitted, the first Negro to kill a
white in Mississippi and go free after a trial. But on
Christmas Day 1875, Caldwell was shot to death by a
white gang. It was a sign. The old white rulers were
taking back political power in Mississippi, and everywhere else in the South.

As white violence rose in the 1870s, the national government, even under President Grant, became less enthusiastic about defending blacks, and certainly not prepared to arm them. The Supreme Court played its gyroscopic role of pulling the other branches of government back to more conservative directions when they went too far. It began interpreting the Fourteenth Amendment—passed presumably for racial equality—in a way that made it impotent for this purpose. In 1883, the Civil Rights Act of 1875, outlawing discrimination against Negroes using public facilities, was nullified by the Supreme Court, which said: "Individual invasion of individual rights is not the subject-matter of the amendment." The Fourteenth Amendment, it said, was aimed at state action only. "No state shall . . ."

A remarkable dissent was written by Supreme Court Justice John Harlan, himself a former slaveowner in Kentucky, who said there was Constitutional justification for banning private discrimination. He noted that the Thirteenth Amendment, which banned slavery, applied to individual plantation owners, not just the state. He then argued that discrimination was a badge of slavery and similarly outlawable. He pointed also to the first clause of the Fourteenth Amendment, saying that anyone born in the United States was a citizen, and to the clause in Article 4, Section 2, saying "the citizens of each State shall be entitled to all privileges and immunities of citizens in the several States."

Harlan was fighting a force greater than logic or justice; the mood of the Court reflected a new coalition of northern industrialists and southern businessmen-planters. The culmination of this mood came in the decision of 1896, *Plessy* v. *Ferguson,* when the Court ruled that a railroad could segregate black and white if the segregated facilities were equal:

> The object of the amendment was undoubtedly to enforce the absolute equality of the two races before the law, but in the nature of things it could not have been intended to abolish distinctions based upon color, or to enforce social, as distinguished from political equality, or a commingling of the two races upon terms unsatisfactory to either.

Harlan again dissented: "Our Constitution is color-blind. . . ."

It was the year 1877 that spelled out clearly and dramatically what was happening. When the year opened, the presidential election of the past November was in bitter dispute. The Democratic candidate, Samuel Tilden, had 184 votes and needed one more to be elected: his popular vote was greater by 250,000. The Republican candidate, Rutherford Hayes, had 166 electoral votes. Three states not yet counted had a total of 19 electoral votes; if Hayes could get all of those, he would have 185 and be President. This is what his managers proceeded to arrange. They made concessions to the Democratic party and the white South, including an agreement to remove Union troops from the South, the last military obstacle to the reestablishment of white supremacy there.

Northern political and economic interests needed powerful allies and stability in the face of national crisis. The country had been in economic depression since 1873, and by 1877 farmers and workers were beginning to rebel. As C. Vann Woodward puts it in his history of the 1877 Compromise, *Reunion and Reaction:*

> It was a depression year, the worst year of the severest depression yet experienced. In the East labor and the unemployed were in a bitter and violent temper. . . . Out West a tide of agrarian radicalism was rising. . . . From both East and West came threats against the elaborate structure of protective tariffs, national banks, railroad subsidies and monetary arrangements upon which the new economic order was founded.

It was a time for reconciliation between southern and northern elites. Woodward asks: " . . . could the South be induced to combine with the Northern conservatives and become a prop instead of a menace to the new capitalist order?"

With billions of dollars' worth of slaves gone, the wealth of the old South was wiped out. They now looked to the national government for help: credit, subsidies, flood control projects. The United States in 1865 had spent $103,294,501 on public works, but the South received only $9,469,363. For instance, while Ohio got over a million dollars, Kentucky, her neighbor south of the river, got $25,000. While Maine got $3 million, Mississippi got $136,000. While $83 million had been given to subsidize the Union Pacific and Central Pacific railroads, thus creating a transcontinental railroad through the

North, there was no such subsidy for the South. So one of the things the South looked for was federal aid to the Texas and Pacific Railroad.

Woodward says: "By means of appropriations, subsidies, grants, and bonds such as Congress had so lavishly showered upon capitalist enterprise in the North, the South might yet mend its fortunes—or at any rate the fortunes of a privileged elite." These privileges were sought with the backing of poor white farmers, brought into the new alliance against blacks. The farmers wanted railroads, harbor improvements, flood control, and, of course, land—not knowing yet how these would be used not to help them but to exploit them.

For example, as the first act of the new North-South capitalist cooperation, the Southern Homestead Act, which had reserved all federal lands— one-third of the area of Alabama, Arkansas, Florida, Louisiana, Mississippi—for farmers who would work the land, was repealed. This enabled absentee speculators and lumbermen to move in and buy up much of this land.

And so the deal was made. The proper committee was set up by both houses of Congress to decide where the electoral votes would go. The decision was: they belonged to Hayes, and he was now President.

As Woodward sums it up:

> The Compromise of 1877 did not restore the old order in the South. . . . It did assure the dominant whites political autonomy and non-intervention in matters of race policy and promised them a share

in the blessings of the new economic order. In return, the South became, in effect, a satellite of the dominant region. . . .

The importance of the new capitalism in over-turning what black power existed in the postwar South is affirmed by Horace Mann Bond's study of Alabama Reconstruction, which shows, after 1868, "a struggle between different financiers." Yes, racism was a factor but "accumulations of capital, and the men who controlled them, were as unaffected by attitudinal prejudices as it is possible to be. Without sentiment, without emotion, those who sought profit from an exploitation of Alabama's natural resources turned other men's prejudices and attitudes to their own account, and did so with skill and a ruthless acumen."

It was an age of coal and power, and northern Alabama had both. "The bankers in Philadelphia and New York, and even in London and Paris, had known this for almost two decades. The only thing lacking was transportation." And so, in the mid-1870s, Bond notes, northern bankers began appearing in the directories of southern railroad lines. J. P. Morgan appears by 1875 as director for several lines in Alabama and Georgia.

In the year 1886, Henry Grady, an editor of the Atlanta *Constitution*, spoke at a dinner in New York. In the audience were J. P. Morgan, H. M. Flagler (an associate of Rockefeller), Russell Sage, and Charles Tiffany. His talk was called "The New South" and his theme was: Let bygones be bygones; let us have a new era of peace and prosperity; the Negro was a prosperous laboring class; he had the fullest protection of the laws and the friendship of the southern people. Grady joked about the northerners who sold slaves to the South and said the South could now handle its own race problem. He received a rising ovation, and the band played "Dixie."

That same month, an article in the New York *Daily Tribune:*

> The leading coal and iron men of the South, who have been in this city during the last ten days, will go home to spend the Christmas holidays, thoroughly satisfied with the business of the year, and more than hopeful for the future. And they have good reason to be. The time for which they have been waiting for nearly twenty years, when Northern capitalists would be convinced not only of the safety but of the immense profits to be gained from the investment of their money in developing the fabulously rich coal and iron resources of Alabama, Tennessee, and Georgia, has come at last.

The North, it must be recalled, did not have to undergo a revolution in its thinking to accept the subordination of the Negro. When the Civil War ended, nineteen of the twenty-four northern states did not allow blacks to vote. By 1900, all the southern states, in new constitutions and new statutes, had written into law the disfranchisement and segregation of Negroes, and a *New York Times* editorial said: "Northern men . . . no longer denounce the suppression of the Negro vote. . . . The necessity of it under the supreme law of self-preservation is candidly recognized."

While not written into law in the North, the counterpart in racist thought and practice was there. An item in the Boston *Transcript*, September 25, 1895:

A colored man who gives his name as Henry W. Turner was arrested last night on suspicion of being a highway robber. He was taken this morning to Black's studio, where he had his picture taken for the "Rogue's Gallery". That angered him, and he made himself as disagreeable as he possibly could. Several times along the way to the photographer's he resisted the police with all his might, and had to be clubbed.

In the postwar literature, images of the Negro came mostly from southern white writers like Thomas Nelson Page, who in his novel *Red Rock* referred to a Negro character as "a hyena in a cage," "a reptile," "a species of worm," "a wild beast." And, interspersed with paternalistic urgings of friendship for the Negro, Joel Chandler Harris, in his Uncle Remus stories, would have Uncle Remus say: "Put a spellin-book in a nigger's han's, en right den en dar' you loozes a plowhand. I kin take a bar'l stave an fling mo' sense inter a nigger in one minnit dan all de schoolhouses betwixt dis en de state er Midgigin."

In this atmosphere it was no wonder that those Negro leaders most accepted in white society, like the educator Booker T. Washington, a one-time White House guest of Theodore Roosevelt, urged Negro political passivity. Invited by the white organizers of the Cotton States and International Exposition in Atlanta in 1895 to speak, Washington urged the southern Negro to "cast down your bucket where you are"—that is, to stay in the South, to be farmers, mechanics, domestics, perhaps even to attain to the professions. He urged white employers to hire Negroes rather than immigrants of "strange tongue and habits." Negroes, "without strikes and labor wars," were the "most patient, faithful, law-abiding and unresentful people that the world has seen." He said: "The wisest among my race understand that the agitation of questions of social equality is the extremest folly."

Perhaps Washington saw this as a necessary tactic of survival in a time of hangings and burnings of Negroes throughout the South. It was a low point for black people in America. Thomas Fortune, a young black editor of the New York *Globe,* testified before a Senate committee in 1883 about the situation of the Negro in the United States. He spoke of "widespread poverty," of government betrayal, of desperate Negro attempts to educate themselves.

The average wage of Negro farm laborers in the South was about fifty cents a day, Fortune said. He was usually paid in "orders," not money, which he could use only at a store controlled by the planter, "a system of fraud." The Negro farmer, to get the wherewithal to plant his crop, had to promise it to the store, and when everything was added up at the end of the year he was in debt, so his crop was constantly owed to someone, and he was tied to the land, with the records kept by the planter and storekeeper so that the Negroes "are swindled and kept forever in debt." As for supposed laziness, "I am surprised that a larger number of them do not go to fishing, hunting, and loafing."

Fortune spoke of "the penitentiary system of the South, with its infamous chain-gang. . . . the object being to terrorize the blacks and furnish victims for contractors, who purchase the labor of these wretches from the State for a song. . . . The white man who shoots a negro always goes free, while the negro who steals a hog is sent to the chain-gang for ten years."

Many Negroes fled. About six thousand black people left Texas, Louisiana, and Mississippi and migrated to Kansas to escape violence and poverty. Frederick Douglass and some other leaders thought this was a wrong tactic, but migrants rejected such advice. "We have found no leader to trust but God overhead of us," one said. Henry Adams, another black migrant, illiterate, a veteran of the Union army, told a Senate committee in 1880 why he left Shreveport, Louisiana: "We seed that the whole South—every state in the South—had got into the hands of the very men that held us slaves."

Even in the worst periods, southern Negroes continued to meet, to organize in self-defense. Herbert Aptheker reprints thirteen documents of meetings, petitions, and appeals of Negroes in the 1880s—in Baltimore, Louisiana, the Carolinas, Virginia, Georgia, Florida, Texas, Kansas—showing the spirit of defiance and resistance of blacks all over the South. This, in the face of over a hundred lynchings a year by this time.

Despite the apparent hopelessness of this situation, there were black leaders who thought Booker T. Washington wrong in advocating caution and moderation. John Hope, a young black man in Georgia, who heard Washington's Cotton Exposition speech,

told students at a Negro college in Nashville, Tennessee:

> If we are not striving for equality, in heaven's
> name for what are we living? I regard it as cow-
> ardly and dishonest for any of our colored men to
> tell white people or colored people that we are not
> struggling for equality. . . . Yes, my friends, I want
> equality. Nothing less. . . . Now catch your breath,
> for I am going to use an adjective: I am going to
> say we demand social equality. . . . I am no wild
> beast, nor am I an unclean thing.
>
> Rise, Brothers! Come let us possess this land.
> . . . Be discontented. Be dissatisfied. . . . Be as
> restless as the tempestuous billows on the bound-
> less sea. Let your discontent break mountain-high
> against the wall of prejudice, and swamp it to the
> very foundation. . . .

Another black man, who came to teach at Atlanta University, W.E.B. DuBois, saw the late-
nineteenth-century betrayal of the Negro as part
of a larger happening in the United States, something happening not only to poor blacks but to
poor whites. In his book *Black Reconstruction*, written in 1935, he said:

> God wept; but that mattered little to an unbeliev-
> ing age; what mattered most was that the world
> wept and still is weeping and blind with tears and
> blood. For there began to rise in America in 1876
> a new capitalism and a new enslavement of labor.

DuBois saw this new capitalism as part of a process of exploitation and bribery taking place in all the "civilized" countries of the world:

> Home labor in cultured lands, appeased and misled by a ballot whose power the dictatorship of vast capital strictly curtailed, was bribed by high wage and political office to unite in an exploitation of white, yellow, brown and black labor, in lesser lands. . . .

Was DuBois right—that in that growth of American capitalism, before and after the Civil War, whites as well as blacks were in some sense becoming slaves?

2

The Other Civil War

A sheriff in the Hudson River Valley near Albany, New York, about to go into the hills in the fall of 1839 to collect back rents from tenants on the enormous Rensselaer estate, was handed a letter:

> . . . the tenants have organized themselves into a body, and resolved not to pay any more rent until they can be redressed of their grievances. . . . The tenants now assume the right of doing to their landlord as he has for a long time done with them, viz: as they please.
>
> You need not think this to be children's play. . . . if you come out in your official capacity . . . I would not pledge for your safe return. . . . A Tenant.

When a deputy arrived in the farming area with writs demanding the rent, farmers suddenly appeared, assembled by the blowing of tin horns. They seized his writs and burned them.

That December, a sheriff and a mounted posse of five hundred rode into the farm country, but found themselves in the midst of shrieking tin horns, eighteen hundred farmers blocking their path, six hundred more blocking their rear, all mounted, armed with pitchforks and clubs. The sheriff and his posse turned back, the rear guard parting to let them through.

This was the start of the Anti-Renter movement in the Hudson Valley, described by Henry Christman in *Tin Horns and Calico.* It was a protest against the patroonship system, which went back to the 1600s when the Dutch ruled New York, a system where (as Christman describes it) "a few families, intricately intermarried, controlled the destinies of three hundred thousand people and ruled in almost kingly splendor near two million acres of land."

The tenants paid taxes and rents. The largest manor was owned by the Rensselaer family, which ruled over about eighty thousand tenants and had accumulated a fortune of $41 million. The landowner, as one sympathizer of the tenants put it, could "swill his wine, loll on his cushions, fill his life with society, food, and culture, and ride his barouche and five saddle horses along the beautiful river valley and up to the backdrop of the mountain."

By the summer of 1839, the tenants were holding their first mass meeting. The economic crisis of 1837 had filled the area with unemployed seeking land, on top of the layoffs accompanying the completion of the Erie Canal, after the first wave of railroad building ended. That summer the tenants resolved: "We will take up the ball of the Revolution where our fathers stopped it and roll it to the final consummation of freedom and independence of the masses."

Certain men in the farm country became leaders and organizers: Smith Boughton, a country doctor on horseback; Ainge Devyr, a revolutionary Irishman. Devyr had seen monopoly of land and industry bring misery to the slumdwellers of London, Liverpool, and Glasgow, had agitated for change, had been arrested for sedition, and fled to America. He was invited to address a Fourth of July rally of farmers in Rensselaerville, where he warned his listeners: "If you permit unprincipled and ambitious men to monopolize the soil, they will become masters of the country in the certain order of cause and effect. . . ."

Thousands of farmers in Rensselaer country were organized into Anti-Renter associations to prevent the landlords from evicting. They agreed on calico Indian costumes, symbol of the Boston Tea Party and recalling original ownership of the soil. The tin horn represented an Indian call to arms. Soon ten thousand men were trained and ready.

Organizing went on in county after county, in dozens of towns along the Hudson. Handbills appeared:

ATTENTION
ANTI-RENTERS! AWAKE! AROUSE! . . .
Strike till the last armed foe expires,
Strike for your altars and your fires—

Strike for the green graves of your sires,
God and your happy homes!

Sheriffs and deputy sheriffs trying to serve writs
on farmers were surrounded by calico-clad riders
who had been summoned by tin horns sounding in
the countryside—then tarred and feathered. The
New York *Herald,* once sympathetic, now deplored
"the insurrectionary spirit of the mountaineers."

One of the most hated elements of the lease gave
the landlord the right to the timber on all the farms.
A man sent onto a tenant's land to gather wood for
the landlord was killed. Tension rose. A farm boy was
killed mysteriously, no one knew by whom, but Dr.
Boughton was jailed. The governor ordered artillery-
men into action, and a company of cavalry came up
from New York City.

Petitions for an anti-rent bill, signed by 25,000
tenants, were put before the legislature in 1845. The
bill was defeated. A kind of guerrilla war resumed in
the country, between bands of "Indians" and sheriffs' posses. Boughton was kept in jail seven months,
four and a half months of that in heavy irons, before
being released on bail. Fourth of July meetings in
1845 attended by thousands of farmers pledged continued resistance.

When a deputy sheriff tried to sell the livestock
of a farmer named Moses Earle, who owed $60
rent on 160 stony acres, there was a fight, and the
deputy was killed. Similar attempts to sell livestock
for rent payments were thwarted, again and again.
The governor sent three hundred troops in, declaring a state of rebellion existed, and soon almost

a hundred Anti-Renters were in jail. Smith Boughton was brought to trial. He was charged with taking papers from a sheriff but declared by the judge
to have in fact committed "high treason, rebellion
against your government, and armed insurrection"
and sentenced to life imprisonment.

Those "Indians" found to be armed and disguised at Moses Earle's farm, where the deputy had
been killed, were declared by the judge to be guilty
of murder, and the jury was so instructed. All were
found guilty, and the judge sentenced four to life imprisonment and two to be hanged. Two of the leaders were told to write letters urging the Anti-Renters
to disband, as their only chance to escape heavy sentences. They wrote the letters.

The power of the law thus crushed the Anti-
Renter movement. It was intended to make clear
that farmers could not win by fighting—that they
must confine their efforts to voting, to acceptable
methods of reform. In 1845, the Anti-Renters elected
fourteen members to the state legislature. Governor
Silas Wright now commuted to life imprisonment
the two death sentences and asked the legislature to
give relief to the tenants, to end the feudal system in
the Hudson Valley. Proposals to break up the huge
estates on the death of the owners were defeated,
but the legislature voted to make illegal the selling
of tenant property for nonpayment of rent. A constitutional convention that year outlawed new feudal
leases.

The next governor, elected in 1846 with Anti-
Renter support, had promised to pardon the Anti-
Renter prisoners, and he did. Throngs of farmers

greeted them on their release. Court decisions in the 1850s began to limit the worst features of the manorial system, without changing the fundamentals of landlord-tenant relations.

Sporadic farmer resistance to the collection of back rents continued into the 1860s. As late as 1869, bands of "Indians" were still assembling to thwart sheriffs acting for a rich valley landowner named Walter Church. In the early 1880s a deputy sheriff trying to dispossess a farmer on behalf of Church was killed by shotgun fire. By this time most leases had passed into the hands of the farmers. In three of the main Anti-Renter counties, of twelve thousand farmers, only two thousand remained under lease.

The farmers had fought, been crushed by the law, their struggle diverted into voting, and the system stabilized by enlarging the class of small landowners, leaving the basic structure of rich and poor intact. It was a common sequence in American history.

Around the time of the Anti-Renter movement in New York, there was excitement in Rhode Island over Dorr's Rebellion. As Marvin Gettleman points out in *The Dorr Rebellion,* it was both a movement for electoral reform and an example of radical insurgency. It was prompted by the Rhode Island charter's rule that only owners of land could vote.

As more people left the farm for the city, as immigrants came to work in the mills, the disfranchised grew. Seth Luther, self-educated carpenter in Providence and spokesman for working people, wrote in 1833 the "Address on the Right of Free Suffrage," denouncing the monopoly of political power by "the mushroom lordlings, sprigs of nobility . . . small potato aristocrats" of Rhode Island. He urged non-cooperation with the government, refusing to pay taxes or to serve in the militia. Why, he asked, should twelve thousand working people in Rhode Island without the vote submit to five thousand who had land and could vote?

Thomas Dorr, a lawyer from a well-to-do family, became a leader of the suffrage movement. Working people formed the Rhode Island Suffrage Association, and in the spring of 1841 thousands paraded in Providence carrying banners and signs for electoral reform. Going outside the legal system, they organized their own "People's Convention" and drafted a new constitution without property qualifications for voting.

In early 1842, they invited votes on the constitution; fourteen thousand voted for it, including about five thousand with property—therefore a majority even of those legally entitled to vote by the charter. In April they held an unofficial election, in which Dorr ran unopposed for governor, and six thousand people voted for him. The governor of Rhode Island in the meantime got the promise of President John Tyler that in the case of rebellion federal troops would be sent. There was a clause in the U.S. Constitution to meet just that kind of situation, providing for federal intervention to quell local insurrections on request of a state government.

Ignoring this, on May 3, 1842, the Dorr forces held an inauguration with a great parade of artisans, shopkeepers, mechanics, and militia marching through Providence. The newly elected People's

Legislature was convened. Dorr led a fiasco of an attack on the state arsenal, his cannon misfiring. Dorr's arrest was ordered by the regular governor, and he went into hiding outside the state, trying to raise military support.

Despite the protests of Dorr and a few others, the "People's Constitution" kept the word "white" in its clause designating voters. Angry Rhode Island blacks now joined the militia units of the Law and Order coalition, which promised that a new constitutional convention would give them the right to vote.

When Dorr returned to Rhode Island, he found several hundred of his followers, mostly working people, willing to fight for the People's Constitution, but there were thousands in the regular militia on the side of the state. The rebellion disintegrated and Dorr again fled Rhode Island.

Martial law was declared. One rebel soldier, captured, was blindfolded and put before a firing squad, which fired with blank bullets. A hundred other militia were taken prisoner. One of them described their being bound by ropes into platoons of eight, marched on foot 16 miles to Providence, "threatened and pricked by the bayonet if we lagged from fatigue, the rope severely chafing our arms; the skin off mine. . . . no water till we reached Greenville . . . no food until the next day. . . . and, after being exhibited, were put into the State prison."

A new constitution offered some reform. It still gave overrepresentation to the rural areas, limited the vote to property owners or those who paid a one-dollar poll tax, and would let naturalized citizens vote only if they had $134 in real estate. In the elections of early 1843, the Law and Order group, opposed by former Dorrites, used intimidation of state militia, of employees by employers, of tenants by landlords, to get out their vote. It lost in the industrial towns, but got the vote of the agrarian areas, and won all major offices.

Dorr returned to Rhode Island in the fall of 1843. He was arrested on the streets of Providence and tried for treason. The jury, instructed by the judge to ignore all political arguments and consider only whether Dorr had committed certain overt acts (which he never denied committing), found him guilty, whereupon the judge sentenced him to life imprisonment at hard labor. He spent twenty months in jail, and then a newly elected Law and Order governor, anxious to end Dorr's martyrdom, pardoned him.

Armed force had failed, the ballot had failed, the courts had taken the side of the conservatives. The Dorr movement now went to the U.S. Supreme Court, via a trespass suit by Martin Luther against Law and Order militiamen, charging that the People's Government was the legitimate government in Rhode Island in 1842. Daniel Webster argued against the Dorrites. If people could claim a constitutional right to overthrow an existing government, Webster said, there would be no more law and no more government; there would be anarchy.

In its decision, the Supreme Court established (*Luther* v. *Borden,* 1849) a long-lasting doctrine: it would not interfere in certain "political" questions, to be left to executive and legislature. The decision reinforced the essentially conservative nature of the

Supreme Court: that on critical issues—war and revolution—it would defer to the President and Congress.

The stories of the Anti-Renter movement and
Dorr's Rebellion are not usually found in textbooks
on United States history. In these books, given to
millions of young Americans, there is little on class
struggle in the nineteenth century. The period before and after the Civil War is filled with politics,
elections, slavery, and the race question. Even where
specialized books on the Jacksonian period deal
with labor and economic issues they center on the
presidency, and thus perpetuate the traditional de-
pendency on heroic leaders rather than people's
struggles.

Andrew Jackson said he spoke for "the humble
members of society—the farmer, mechanics and laborers. . . ." He certainly did not speak for the Indians being pushed off their lands, or slaves. But the
tensions aroused by the developing factory system,
the growing immigration, required that the government develop a mass base of support among whites.
"Jacksonian Democracy" did just that.

Politics in this period of the 1830s and 1840s, according to Douglas Miller, a specialist in the Jacksonian period *(The Birth of Modern America)*, "had
become increasingly centered around creating a
popular image and flattering the common man."
Miller is dubious, however, about the accuracy of
that phrase "Jacksonian Democracy":

> Parades, picnics, and campaigns of personal slan-
> der characterized Jacksonian politicking. But, al-

though both parties aimed their rhetoric at the people and mouthed the sacred shibboleths of democracy, this did not mean that the common man ruled America. The professional politicians coming to the fore in the twenties and thirties, though sometimes self-made, were seldom ordinary. Both major parties were controlled largely by men of wealth and ambition. Lawyers, newspaper editors, merchants, industrialists, large landowners, and speculators dominated the Democrats as well as the Whigs.

Jackson was the first President to master the liberal rhetoric—to speak for the common man. This was a necessity for political victory when the vote was being demanded—as in Rhode Island—by more and more people, and state legislatures were loosening voting restrictions. As another Jacksonian scholar, Robert Remini (*The Age of Jackson*), says, after studying electoral figures for 1828 and 1832:

> Jackson himself enjoyed widespread support that ranged across all classes and sections of the country. He attracted farmers, mechanics, laborers, professionals and even businessmen. And all this without Jackson being clearly pro- or antilabor, pro- or antibusiness, pro- or antilower, middle or upper class. It has been demonstrated that he was a strikebreaker [Jackson sent troops to control rebellious workers on the Chesapeake and Ohio Canal], yet at different times . . . he and the Democrats received the backing of organized labor.

It was the new politics of ambiguity—speaking
for the lower and middle classes to get their support
in times of rapid growth and potential turmoil. The
two-party system came into its own in this time. To
give people a choice between two different parties
and allow them, in a period of rebellion, to choose the
slightly more democratic one was an ingenious mode
of control. Like so much in the American system, it
was not devilishly contrived by some master plotters;
it developed naturally out of the needs of the situation. Remini compares the Jacksonian Democrat Martin Van Buren, who succeeded Jackson as President,
with the Austrian conservative statesman Metternich:
"Like Metternich, who was seeking to thwart revolutionary discontent in Europe, Van Buren and similar
politicians were attempting to banish political disorder
from the United States by a balance of power achieved
through two well-organized and active parties."

The Jacksonian idea was to achieve stability and
control by winning to the Democratic party "the
middling interest, and especially . . . the substantial
yeomanry of the country" by "prudent, judicious,
well-considered reform." That is, reform that would
not yield too much. These were the words of Robert
Rantoul, a reformer, corporation lawyer, and Jacksonian Democrat. It was a forecast of the successful
appeal of the Democratic party—and at times the
Republican party—in the twentieth century.

Such new forms of political control were needed
in the turbulence of growth, the possibility of rebellion. Now there were canals, railroads, the tele-
graph. In 1790, fewer than a million Americans
lived in cities; in 1840 the figure was 11 million. New

York had 130,000 people in 1820, a million by 1860. And while the traveler Alexis de Tocqueville had expressed astonishment at "the general equality of condition among the people," he was not very good at numbers, his friend Beaumont said. And his observation was not in accord with the facts, according to Edward Pessen, a historian of Jacksonian society (*Jacksonian America*).

In Philadelphia, working-class families lived fifty-five to a tenement, usually one room per family, with no garbage removal, no toilets, no fresh air or water. There was fresh water newly pumped from the Schuylkill River, but it was going to the homes of the rich.

In New York you could see the poor lying in the streets with the garbage. There were no sewers in the slums, and filthy water drained into yards and alleys, into the cellars where the poorest of the poor lived, bringing with it a typhoid epidemic in 1837, typhus in 1842. In the cholera epidemic of 1832, the rich fled the city; the poor stayed and died.

These poor could not be counted on as political allies of the government. But they were there—like slaves, or Indians—invisible ordinarily, a menace if they rose. There were more solid citizens, however, who might give steady support to the system—better-paid workers, landowning farmers. Also, there was the new urban white-collar worker, born in the rising commerce of the time, described by Thomas Cochran and William Miller (*The Age of Enterprise*):

> Dressed in drab alpaca, hunched over a high desk, this new worker credited and debited, indexed

and filed, wrote and stamped invoices, accep-
tances, bills of lading, receipts. Adequately paid,
he had some extra money and leisure time. He
patronized sporting events and theaters, savings
banks and insurance companies. He read Day's
New York Sun or Bennett's *Herald*—the "penny
press" supported by advertising, filled with police
reports, crime stories, etiquette advice for the rising bourgeoisie. . . .

This was the advance guard of a growing class
of white-collar workers and professionals in America
who would be wooed enough and paid enough to
consider themselves members of the bourgeois class,
and to give support to that class in times of crisis.

The opening of the West was being helped by
mechanization of the farm. Iron plows cut plowing
time in half; by the 1850s John Deere Company
was turning out ten thousand plows a year. Cyrus
McCormick was making a thousand mechanical
reapers a year in his factory in Chicago. A man
with a sickle could cut half an acre of wheat in a
day; with a reaper he could cut 10 acres.

Turnpikes, canals, and railroads were bringing
more people west, more products east, and it became important to keep that new West, tumultuous
and unpredictable, under control. When colleges
were established out West, eastern businessmen, as
Cochran and Miller say, were "determined from the
start to control western education." Edward Ever-
ett, the Massachusetts politician and orator, spoke
in 1833 on behalf of giving financial aid to western
colleges:

Let no Boston capitalist, then, let no man, who has
a large stake in New England. . . think that he is
called upon to exercise his liberality at a distance,
toward those in whom he has no concern. . . . They
ask you to give security to your own property, by
diffusing the means of light and truth throughout
the region, where so much of the power to preserve or to shake it resides. . . .

The capitalists of the East were conscious of the
need for this "security to your own property." As
technology developed, more capital was needed,
more risks had to be taken, and a big investment
needed stability. In an economic system not rationally
planned for human need, but developing fitfully,
chaotically out of the profit motive, there seemed
to be no way to avoid recurrent booms and slumps.
There was a slump in 1837, another in 1853. One
way to achieve stability was to decrease competition,
organize the businesses, move toward monopoly. In
the mid-1850s, price agreements and mergers became frequent: the New York Central Railroad was
a merger of many railroads. The American Brass
Association was formed "to meet ruinous competition," it said. The Hampton County Cotton Spinners
Association was organized to control prices, and so
was the American Iron Association.

Another way to minimize risks was to make sure
the government played its traditional role, going
back to Alexander Hamilton and the first Congress,
of helping the business interests. State legislatures
gave charters to corporations giving them legal
rights to conduct business, raise money—at first

special charters, then general charters, so that any business meeting certain requirements could incorporate. Between 1790 and 1860, 2,300 corporations were chartered.

Railroad men traveled to Washington and to state capitals armed with money, shares of stock, free railroad passes. Between 1850 and 1857 they got 25 million acres of public land, free of charge, and millions of dollars in bonds—loans—from the state legislatures. In Wisconsin in 1856, the LaCrosse and Milwaukee Railroad got a million acres free by distributing about $900,000 in stocks and bonds to fifty-nine assemblymen, thirteen senators, the governor. Two years later the railroad was bankrupt and the bonds were worthless.

In the East, mill owners had become powerful, and organized. By 1850, fifteen Boston families called the "Associates" controlled 20 percent of the cotton spindleage in the United States, 39 percent of insurance capital in Massachusetts, 40 percent of banking resources in Boston.

In the schoolbooks, those years are filled with the controversy over slavery, but on the eve of the Civil War it was money and profit, not the movement against slavery, that was uppermost in the priorities of the men who ran the country. As Cochran and Miller put it:

> Webster was the hero of the North—not Emerson, Parker, Garrison, or Phillips; Webster the tariff man, the land speculator, the corporation lawyer, politician for the Boston Associates, inheritor of Hamilton's coronet. "The great object of govern-

ment" said he "is the protection of property at home, and respect and renown abroad." For these he preached union; for these he surrendered the fugitive slave.

They describe the Boston rich:

Living sumptuously on Beacon Hill, admired by their neighbors for their philanthropy and their patronage of art and culture, these men traded in State Street while overseers ran their factories, managers directed their railroads, agents sold their water power and real estate. They were absentee landlords in the most complete sense. Uncontaminated by the diseases of the factory town, they were also protected from hearing the complaints of their workers or suffering mental depression from dismal and squalid surroundings. In the metropolis, art, literature, education, science, flowered in the Golden Day; in the industrial towns children went to work with their fathers and mothers, schools and doctors were only promises, a bed of one's own was a rare luxury.

Ralph Waldo Emerson described Boston in those years: "There is a certain poor-smell in all the streets, in Beacon Street and Mount Vernon, as well as in the lawyers' offices, and the wharves, and the same meanness and sterility, and leave-all-hope-behind, as one finds in a boot manufacturer's premises." The preacher Theodore Parker told his congregation: "Money is this day the strongest power of the nation."

The attempts at political stability, at economic control, did not quite work. The new industrialism, the crowded cities, the long hours in the factories, the sudden economic crises leading to high prices and lost jobs, the lack of food and water, the freezing winters, the hot tenements in the summer, the epidemics of disease, the deaths of children—these led to sporadic reactions from the poor. Sometimes there were spontaneous, unorganized uprisings against the rich. Sometimes the anger was deflected into racial hatred for blacks, religious warfare against Catholics, nativist fury against immigrants. Sometimes it was organized into demonstrations and strikes.

"Jacksonian Democracy" had tried to create a consensus of support for the system to make it secure. Blacks, Indians, women, and foreigners were clearly outside the consensus. But also, white working people, in large numbers, declared themselves outside.

The full extent of the working-class consciousness of those years—as of any years—is lost in history, but fragments remain and make us wonder how much of this always existed underneath the very practical silence of working people. In 1827 an "Address . . . before the Mechanics and Working Classes . . . of Philadelphia" was recorded, written by an "Unlettered Mechanic," probably a young shoemaker, who said:

> We find ourselves oppressed on every hand—we
> labor hard in producing all the comforts of life for
> the enjoyment of others, while we ourselves obtain

THE OTHER CIVIL WAR 87

but a scanty portion, and even that in the present
state of society depends on the will of employers.

Frances Wright of Scotland, an early feminist
and Utopian socialist, was invited by Philadelphia
workingmen to speak on the Fourth of July 1829 to
one of the first city-wide associations of labor unions
in the United States. She asked if the Revolution had
been fought "to crush down the sons and daughters
of your country's industry under . . . neglect, poverty,
vice, starvation, and disease. . . ." She wondered if the
new technology was not lowering the value of human
labor, making people appendages to machines, crip-
pling the minds and bodies of child laborers.

Later that year, George Henry Evans, a printer,
editor of the *Workingman's Advocate,* wrote "The Working Men's Declaration of Independence." Among its
list of "facts" submitted to "candid and impartial" fellow citizens:

1. The laws for levying taxes are . . . operating most
   oppressively on one class of society. . . .
3. The laws for private incorporation are all partial
   . . . favoring one class of society to the expense of the
   other. . . .
6. The laws . . . have deprived nine tenths of
   the members of the body politics, who are not
   wealthy, of the equal means to enjoy "life, liberty,
   and the pursuit of happiness." . . . The lien law
   in favor of the landlords against tenants . . . is
   one illustration among innumerable others.

Evans believed that "all on arriving at adult age are entitled to equal property."

A city-wide "Trades' Union" in Boston in 1834, including mechanics from Charlestown and women shoe binders from Lynn, referred to the Declaration of Independence:

> We hold . . . that laws which have a tendency to raise any peculiar class above their fellow citizens, by granting special privileges, are contrary to and in defiance of those primary principles. . . .
>
> Our public system of Education, which so liberally endows those seminaries of learning, which . . . are only accessible to the wealthy, while our common schools . . . are so illy provided for . . . Thus even in childhood the poor are apt to think themselves inferior. . . .

In his book *Most Uncommon Jacksonians*, Edward Pessen says: "The leaders of the Jacksonian labor movement were radicals. . . . How else describe men who believed American society to be torn with social conflict, disfigured by the misery of the masses, and dominated by a greedy elite whose power over every aspect of American life was based on private property?"

Episodes of insurrection of that time have gone unrecorded in traditional histories. Such was the riot in Baltimore in the summer of 1835, when the Bank of Maryland collapsed and its depositors lost their savings. Convinced that a great fraud had taken place, a crowd gathered and began breaking the windows of officials associated with the bank.

When the rioters destroyed a house, the militia attacked, killing some twenty people, wounding a hundred. The next evening, other houses were attacked. The events were reported in *Niles' Weekly Register,* an important newspaper of that time:

> Last night (Sunday) at dark, the attack was renewed upon Reverdy Johnson's house. There was now no opposition. It was supposed that several thousand people were spectators of the scene. The house was soon entered, and its furniture, a very extensive law library, and all its contents, were cast forth, a bonfire made of them in front of the house. The whole interior of the house was torn out and cast upon the burning pile. The marble portico in front, and a great portion of the front wall were torn down by about 11 o'clock. . . . They proceeded to that of the mayor of the city, Jesse Hunt, esq. broke it open, took out the furniture, and burnt it before the door. . . .

During those years, trade unions were forming. (Philip Foner's *History of the Labor Movement in the U.S.* tells the story in rich detail.) The courts called them conspiracies to restrain trade and therefore illegal, as when in New York twenty-five members of the Union Society of Journeymen Tailors were found guilty of "conspiracy to injure trade, riot, assault, battery." The judge, levying fines, said: "In this favored land of law and liberty, the road to advancement is open to all. . . . Every American knows that or ought to know that he has no better friend than the laws and that he needs no artificial combination

for his protection. They are of foreign origin and I
am led to believe mainly upheld by foreigners."

A handbill was then circulated throughout the
city:

The Rich Against the Poor!
Judge Edwards, the tool of the aristocracy, against the
people! Mechanics and workingmen! A deadly blow
has been struck at your liberty! . . . They have established the precedent that workingmen have no right
to regulate the price of labor, or, in other words, the
rich are the only judges of the wants of the poor man.

At City Hall Park, 27,000 people gathered to
denounce the court decision, and elected a Committee of Correspondence which organized, three
months later, a convention of Mechanics, Farmers,
and Working Men, elected by farmers and working people in various towns in New York State. The
convention met in Utica, drew up a Declaration of
Independence from existing political parties, and
established an Equal Rights party.

Although they ran their own candidates for office, there was no great confidence in the ballot as
a way of achieving change. One of the great orators of the movement, Seth Luther, told a Fourth
of July rally: "We will try the ballot box first. If
that will not effect our righteous purpose, the
next and last resort is the cartridge box." And one
sympathetic local newspaper, the Albany *Micro-
scope*, warned:

Remember the regretted fate of the working-men—
they were soon destroyed by hitching teams and
rolling with parties. They admitted into their ranks,
broken down lawyers and politicians. . . . They became perverted, and were unconsciously drawn into
a vortex, from which they never escaped.

The crisis of 1837 led to rallies and meetings in
many cities. The banks had suspended specie payments—refusing to pay hard money for the bank
notes they had issued. Prices rose, and working
people, already hard-pressed to buy food, found that
flour that had sold at $5.62 a barrel was now $12 a
barrel. Pork went up. Coal went up. In Philadelphia,
twenty thousand people assembled, and someone
wrote to President Van Buren describing it:

This afternoon, the largest public meeting I ever
saw assembled in Independence Square. It was
called by placards posted through the city yester-
day and last night. It was projected and carried on
entirely by the working classes; without consulta-
tion or cooperation with any of those who usually
take the lead in such matters. The officers and
speakers were of those classes. . . . It was directed
against the banks.

In New York, members of the Equal Rights party
(often called the Locofocos) announced a meeting:
"Bread, Meat, Rent, and Fuel! Their prices must
come down! The people will meet in the Park, rain or
shine, at 4 o'clock, P.M. on Monday afternoon. . . . All
friends of humanity determined to resist monopolists

and extortioners are invited to attend." The *Commercial Register,* a New York newspaper, reported on the meeting and what followed:

> At 4 o'clock, a concourse of several thousands had convened in front of the City Hall. . . . One of these orators . . . is reported to have expressly directed the popular vengeance against Mr. Eli Hart, who is one of our most extensive flour dealers on commission. "Fellow citizens!" he exclaimed, "Mr. Hart has now 53,000 barrels of flour in his store; let us go and offer him eight dollars a barrel, and if he does not take it . . ."
>
> A large body of the meeting moved off in the direction of Mr. Hart's store . . . the middle door had been forced, and some twenty or thirty barrels of flour or more, rolled into the streets, and the heads staved in. At this point of time, Mr. Hart himself arrived on the ground, with a posse of officers from the police. The officers were assailed by a portion of the mob in Dey Street, their staves wrested from them, and shivered to pieces. . . .
>
> Barrels of flour, by dozens, fifties and hundreds were tumbled into the street from the doors, and thrown in rapid succession from the windows. . . . About one thousand bushels of wheat, and four or five hundred barrels of flour, were thus wantonly and foolishly as well as wickedly destroyed. The most active of the destructionists were foreigners—indeed the greater part of the assemblage was of exotic origin, but there were probably five hundred or a thousand others, standing by and abetting their incendiary labors.

Amidst the falling and bursting of the barrels and sacks of wheat, numbers of women were engaged, like the crones who strip the dead in battle, filling the boxes and baskets with which they were provided, and their aprons, with flour, and making off with it. . . .

Night had now closed upon the scene, but the work of destruction did not cease until strong bodies of police arrived, followed, soon afterward, by detachments of troops. . . .

This was the Flour Riot of 1837. During the crisis of that year, 50,000 persons (one-third of the working class) were without work in New York City alone, and 200,000 (of a population of 500,000) were living, as one observer put it, "in utter and hopeless distress."

There is no complete record of the meetings, riots, actions, organized and disorganized, violent and nonviolent, which took place in the mid-nineteenth century, as the country grew, as the cities became crowded, with working conditions bad, living conditions intolerable, with the economy in the hands of bankers, speculators, landlords, merchants.

In 1835, fifty different trades organized unions in Philadelphia, and there was a successful general strike of laborers, factory workers, bookbinders, jewelers, coal heavers, butchers, cabinet workers—for the ten-hour day. Soon there were ten-hour laws in Pennsylvania and other states, but they provided that employers could have employees sign contracts for longer hours. The law at this time was developing a strong defense of contracts; it was pretended

that work contracts were voluntary agreements between equals.

Weavers in Philadelphia in the early 1840s—mostly
Irish immigrants working at home for employers—
struck for higher wages, attacked the homes of
those refusing to strike, and destroyed their work.
A sheriff's posse tried to arrest some strikers, but
it was broken up by four hundred weavers armed
with muskets and sticks.

Soon, however, antagonism developed between
these Irish Catholic weavers and native-born Prot-
estant skilled workers over issues of religion. In May
1844 there were Protestant-Catholic riots in Kensington, a suburb of Philadelphia; nativist (anti-immigrant)
rioters destroyed the weavers' neighborhoods and attacked a Catholic church. Middle-class politicians soon
led each group into a different political party (the na-
tivists into the American Republican party, the Irish
into the Democratic party), party politics and religion
now substituting for class conflict.

The result of all this, says David Montgomery,
historian of the Kensington Riots, was the fragmen-
tation of the Philadelphia working class. It "thereby
created for historians the illusion of a society lacking
in class conflict," while in reality the class conflicts of
nineteenth-century America "were as fierce as any
known to the industrial world."

The immigrants from Ireland, fleeing starvation
there when the potato crop failed, were coming to
America now, packed into old sailing ships. The stories of these ships differ only in detail from the accounts of the ships that earlier brought black slaves
and later German, Italian, Russian immigrants.

This is a contemporary account of one ship arriving from Ireland, detained at Grosse Isle on the Canadian border:

> On the 18th of May, 1847, the "Urania", from Cork, with several hundred immigrants on board, a large proportion of them sick and dying of the ship-fever, was put into quarantine at Grosse Isle. This was the first of the plague-smitten ships from Ireland which that year sailed up the St. Lawrence. But before the first week of June as many as eighty-four ships of various tonnage were driven in by an easterly wind; and of that enormous number of vessels there was not one free from the taint of malignant typhus, the offspring of famine and of the foul ship-hold. . . . a tolerably quick passage occupied from six to eight weeks. . . .
>
> Who can imagine the horrors of even the shortest passage in an emigrant ship crowded beyond its utmost capacity of stowage with unhappy beings of all ages, with fever raging in their midst . . . the crew sullen or brutal from very desperation, or paralyzed with terror of the plague—the miserable passengers unable to help themselves, or afford the least relief to each other; one-fourth, or one-third, or one-half of the entire number in different stages of the disease; many dying, some dead; the fatal poison intensified by the indescribable foulness of the air breathed and rebreathed by the gasping sufferers—the wails of children, the ravings of the delirious, the cries and groans of those in mortal agony!

> . . . there was no accommodation of any kind
> on the island . . . sheds were rapidly filled with
> the miserable people. . . . Hundreds were literally
> flung on the beach, left amid the mud and stones
> to crawl on the dry land how they could. . . . Many
> of these . . . gasped out their last breath on that
> fatal shore, not able to drag themselves from the
> slime in which they lay. . . .
>
> It was not until the 1st of November that the
> quarantine of Grosse Isle was closed. Upon that
> barren isle as many as 10,000 of the Irish race
> were consigned to the grave-pit. . . .

How could these new Irish immigrants, themselves poor and despised, become sympathizers with
the black slave, who was becoming more and more
the center of attention, the subject of agitation in the
country? Indeed, most working-class activists at this
time ignored the plight of blacks. Ely Moore, a New
York trade union leader elected to Congress, argued
in the House of Representatives against receiving
abolitionist petitions. Racist hostility became an easy
substitute for class frustration.

On the other hand, a white shoemaker wrote in
1848 in the *Awl,* the newspaper of Lynn shoe factory
workers:

> . . . we are nothing but a standing army that keeps
> three million of our brethren in bondage. . . . Liv-
> ing under the shade of Bunker Hill monument,
> demanding in the name of humanity, our right,
> and withholding those rights from others because
> their skin is black! Is it any wonder that God in his

righteous anger has punished us by forcing us to
drink the bitter cup of degradation.

The anger of the city poor often expressed itself in futile violence over nationality or religion.
In New York in 1849 a mob, largely Irish, stormed
the fashionable Astor Place Opera House, where an
English actor, William Charles Macready, was play-
ing Macbeth, in competition with an American actor, Edwin Forrest, who was acting the same role in
another production. The crowd, shouting "Burn the
damn den of aristocracy," charged, throwing bricks.
The militia were called out, and in the violence that
followed about two hundred people were killed or
wounded.

Another economic crisis came in 1857. The
boom in railroads and manufacturing, the surge
of immigration, the increased speculation in stocks
and bonds, the stealing, corruption, manipulation,
led to wild expansion and then crash. By October
of that year, 200,000 were unemployed, and thousands of recent immigrants crowded into the eastern ports, hoping to work their way back to Europe. The *New York Times* reported: "Every ship for
Liverpool now has all the passengers she can carry,
and multitudes are applying to work their passage
if they have no money to pay for it."

In Newark, New Jersey, a rally of several thousand demanded the city give work to the unemployed. And in New York, fifteen thousand people
met at Tompkins Square in downtown Manhat-
tan. From there they marched to Wall Street and
paraded around the Stock Exchange shouting:

"We want work!" That summer, riots occurred in the slum areas of New York. A mob of five hundred attacked the police one day with pistols and bricks. There were parades of the unemployed, demanding bread and work, looting shops. In November, a crowd occupied City Hall, and the U.S. marines were brought in to drive them out.

Of the country's work force of 6 million in 1850, half a million were women: 330,000 worked as domestics; 55,000 were teachers. Of the 181,000 women in factories, half worked in textile mills.

They organized. Women struck by themselves for the first time in 1825. They were the United Tailoresses of New York, demanding higher wages. In 1828, the first strike of mill women on their own took place in Dover, New Hampshire, when several hundred women paraded with banners and flags. They shot off gunpowder, in protest against new factory rules, which charged fines for coming late, forbade talking on the job, and required church attendance. They were forced to return to the mill, their demands unmet, and their leaders were fired and blacklisted.

In Exeter, New Hampshire, women mill workers went on strike ("turned out," in the language of that day) because the overseer was setting the clocks back to get more time from them. Their strike succeeded in exacting a promise from the company that the overseers would set their watches right.

The "Lowell system," in which young girls would go to work in the mills and live in dormitories supervised by matrons, at first seemed beneficent, sociable, a welcome escape from household drudgery or domestic service. Lowell, Massachusetts, was the first town created for the textile mill industry; it was named after the wealthy and influential Lowell family. But the dormitories became prisonlike, controlled by rules and regulations. The supper (served after the women had risen at four in the morning and worked until seven thirty in the evening) often consisted merely of bread and gravy.

So the Lowell girls organized. They started their own newspapers. They protested against the weaving rooms, which were poorly lit, badly ventilated, impossibly hot in the summer, damp and cold in the winter. In 1834, a cut in wages led the Lowell women to strike, proclaiming: "Union is power. Our present object is to have union and exertion, and we remain in possession of our own unquestionable rights. . . ." But the threat of hiring others to replace them brought them back to work at reduced wages (the leaders were fired).

The young women, determined to do better next time, organized a Factory Girls' Association, and 1,500 went on strike in 1836 against a raise in boardinghouse charges. Harriet Hanson was an eleven-year-old girl working in the mill. She later recalled:

I worked in a lower room where I had heard the proposed strike fully, if not vehemently, discussed. I had been an ardent listener to what was said against this attempt at "oppression" on the part of the corporation, and naturally I took sides with the strikers. When the day came on which the girls were to turn out, those in the upper rooms started first, and so many of them left that our

mill was at once shut down. Then, when the girls
in my room stood irresolute, uncertain what to do
. . . I, who began to think they would not go out,
after all their talk, became impatient, and started
on ahead, saying, with childish bravado, "I don't
care what you do, *I* am going to turn out, whether
anyone else does or not," and I marched out, and
was followed by the others.

As I looked back at the long line that followed
me, I was more proud than I have ever been
since. . . .

The strikers marched through the streets of Lowell, singing. They held out a month, but then their
money ran out, they were evicted from the boarding-
houses, and many of them went back to work. The
leaders were fired, including Harriet Hanson's wid-
owed mother, a matron in the boardinghouse, who
was blamed for her child's going out on strike.

Resistance continued. One mill in Lowell, Herbert
Gutman reports, discharged twenty-eight women for
such reasons as "misconduct," "disobedience," "impudence," "levity," and "mutiny." Meanwhile, the
girls tried to hold on to thoughts about fresh air, the
country, a less harried way of life. One of them recalled: "I never cared much for machinery. I could
not see into their complications or feel interested in
them. . . . In sweet June weather I would lean far
out of the window, and try not to hear the unceasing
clash of sound inside."

In New Hampshire, five hundred men and
women petitioned the Amoskeag Manufacturing
Company not to cut down an elm tree to make space

for another mill. They said it was "a beautiful and goodly tree," representing a time "when the yell of the red man and the scream of the eagle were alone heard on the banks of the Merrimack, instead of two giant edifices filled with the buzz of busy and well-remunerated industry."

In 1835, twenty mills went on strike to reduce the workday from thirteen and a half hours to eleven hours, to get cash wages instead of company scrip, and to end fines for lateness. Fifteen hundred children and parents went out on strike, and it lasted six weeks. Strikebreakers were brought in, and some workers went back to work, but the strikers did win a twelve-hour day and nine hours on Saturday. That year and the next, there were 140 strikes in the eastern part of the United States.

The crisis that followed the 1837 panic stimulated the formation in 1845 of the Female Labor Reform Association in Lowell, which sent thousands of petitions to the Massachusetts legislature asking for a ten-hour day. Finally, the legislature decided to hold public hearings, the first investigation of labor conditions by any governmental body in the country. Eliza Hemingway told the committee of the air thick with smoke from oil lamps burning before sunup and after sundown. Judith Payne told of her sickness due to the work in the mills. But after the committee visited the mills—for which the company prepared by a cleanup job—it reported: "Your committee returned fully satisfied that the order, decorum, and general appearance of things in and around the mills could not be improved by any suggestion of theirs or by any act of the legislature."

The report was denounced by the Female Labor
Reform Association, and they worked successfully
for the committee chairman's defeat at the next election, though they could not vote. But not much was
done to change conditions in the mills. In the late
1840s, the New England farm women who worked
in the mills began to leave them, as more and more
Irish immigrants took their place.

Company towns now grew up around mills in
Rhode Island, Connecticut, New Jersey, Pennsylvania, using immigrant workers who signed contracts
pledging everyone in the family to work for a year.
They lived in slum tenements owned by the company,
were paid in scrip, which they could use only at company stores, and were evicted if their work was un-
satisfactory.

In Paterson, New Jersey, the first of a series of
mill strikes was started by children. When the company suddenly put off their dinner hour from noon
to 1:00 P.M., the children marched off the job, their
parents cheering them on. They were joined by other
working people in the town—carpenters, masons,
machinists—who turned the strike into a ten-hour-
day struggle. After a week, however, with the threat
of bringing in militia, the children returned to work,
and their leaders were fired. Soon after, trying to
prevent more trouble, the company restored the
noon dinner hour.

It was the shoemakers of Lynn, Massachusetts,
a factory town northeast of Boston, who started the
largest strike to take place in the United States before the Civil War. Lynn had pioneered in the use of
sewing machines in factories, replacing shoemaker

artisans. The factory workers in Lynn, who began to organize in the 1830s, later started a militant newspaper, the *Awl*. In 1844, four years before Marx and Engels's *Communist Manifesto* appeared, the *Awl* wrote:

> The division of society into the producing and the non-producing classes, and the fact of the unequal distribution of value between the two, introduces us at once to another distinction—that of capital and labor. . . . labor now becomes a commodity. . . . Antagonism and opposition of interest is introduced in the community; capital and labor stand opposed.

The economic crisis of 1857 brought the shoe business to a halt, and the workers of Lynn lost their jobs. There was already anger at machine-stitching replacing shoemakers. Prices were up, wages were repeatedly cut, and by the fall of 1859 men were earning $3 a week and women were earning $1 a week, working sixteen hours a day.

In early 1860, a mass meeting of the newly formed Mechanics Association demanded higher wages. When the manufacturers refused to meet with their committees, the workers called a strike for Washington's Birthday. That morning three thousand shoemakers met in the Lyceum Hall in Lynn and set up committees of 100 to post the names of scabs, to guard against violence, to make sure shoes would not be sent out to be finished elsewhere.

In a few days, shoeworkers throughout New England joined the strike—in Natick, Newbury-

port, Haverhill, Marblehead, and other Massachusetts towns, as well as towns in New Hampshire and
Maine. In a week, strikes had begun in all the shoe
towns of New England, with Mechanics Associations
in twenty-five towns and twenty thousand shoeworkers
on strike. Newspapers called it "The Revolution at
the North," "The Rebellion Among the Workmen of
New England," "Beginning of the Conflict Between
Capital and Labor."

One thousand women and five thousand men
marched through the streets of Lynn in a blizzard,
carrying banners and American flags. Women shoe-
binders and stitchers joined the strike and held their
own mass meeting. A New York *Herald* reporter
wrote of them: "They assail the bosses in a style
which reminds one of the amiable females who par-
ticipated in the first French Revolution." A huge Ladies' Procession was organized, the women marching through streets high with snowdrifts, carrying
signs: "American Ladies Will Not Be Slaves . . . Weak
in Physical Strength but Strong in Moral Courage,
We Dare Battle for the Right, Shoulder to Shoulder
with our Fathers, Husbands, and Brothers." Ten
days after that, a procession of ten thousand striking
workers, including delegations from Salem, Marblehead, and other towns, men and women, marched
through Lynn, in what was the greatest demonstra-
tion of labor to take place in New England up to that
time.

Police from Boston and militia were sent in to
make sure strikers did not interfere with shipments
of shoes to be finished out of the state. The strike
processions went on, while city grocers and provi-

sions dealers provided food for the strikers. The strike continued through March with morale high, but by April it was losing force. The manufacturers offered higher wages to bring the strikers back into the factories, but without recognizing the unions, so that workers still had to face the employer as individuals.

Most of the shoeworkers were native-born Americans, Alan Dawley says in his study of the Lynn strike (*Class and Community*). They did not accept the social and political order that kept them in poverty, however much it was praised in American schools, churches, newspapers. In Lynn, he says, "articulate, activist Irish shoe and leather workers joined Yankees in flatly rejecting the myth of success. Irish and Yankee workers jointly . . . looked for labor candidates when they went to the polls, and resisted strikebreaking by local police." Trying to understand why this fierce class spirit did not lead to independent revolutionary political action, Dawley concludes that the main reason is that electoral politics drained the energies of the resisters into the channels of the system.

Dawley disputes some historians who have said the high rate of mobility of workers prevented them from organizing in revolutionary ways. He says that while there was a high turnover in Lynn too, this "masked the existence of a virtually permanent minority who played the key role in organizing discontent." He also suggests that mobility helps people see that others are in similar conditions. He thinks the struggle of European workers for political democracy, even while they sought economic equality, made them class-conscious. American workers, however, had already gained political democracy by the 1830s, and so their economic battles could be taken over by political parties that blurred class lines.

Even this might not have stopped labor militancy and the rise of class consciousness, Dawley says, if not for the fact that "an entire generation was side-tracked in the 1860's because of the Civil War." Northern wage earners who rallied to the Union cause became allied with their employers. National issues took over from class issues: "At a time when scores of industrial communities like Lynn were seething with resistance to industrialism, national politics were preoccupied with the issues of war and reconstruction." And on these issues the political parties took positions, offered choices, obscured the fact that the political system itself and the wealthy classes it represented were responsible for the problems they now offered to solve.

Class-consciousness was overwhelmed during the Civil War, both North and South, by military and political unity in the crisis of war. That unity was weaned by rhetoric and enforced by arms. It was a war proclaimed as a war for liberty, but working people would be attacked by soldiers if they dared to strike, Indians would be massacred in Colorado by the U.S. army, and those daring to criticize Lincoln's policies would be put in jail without trial—perhaps thirty thousand political prisoners.

Still, there were signs in both sections of dissent from that unity—anger of poor against rich, rebellion against the dominant political and economic forces.

In the North, the war brought high prices for food and the necessities of life. Prices of milk, eggs, cheese were up 60 to 100 percent for families that had not been able to pay the old prices. One historian (Emerson Fite, *Social and Industrial Conditions in the North During the Civil War*) described the war situation: "Employers were wont to appropriate to themselves all or nearly all of the profits accruing from the higher prices, without being willing to grant to the employees a fair share of these profits through the medium of higher wages."

There were strikes all over the country during the war. The Springfield *Republican* in 1863 said that "the workmen of almost every branch of trade have had their strikes within the last few months," and the San Francisco *Evening Bulletin* said "striking for higher wages is now the rage among the working people of San Francisco." Unions were being formed as a result of these strikes. Philadelphia shoemakers in 1863 announced that high prices made organization imperative.

The headline in *Fincher's Trades' Review* of November 21, 1863, "THE REVOLUTION IN NEW YORK," was an exaggeration, but its list of labor activities was impressive evidence of the hidden resentments of the poor during the war:

> The upheaval of the laboring masses in New York has startled the capitalists of that city and vicinity. . . .The machinists are making a bold stand. . . . We publish their appeal in another column.
>
> The City Railroad employees struck for higher wages, and made the whole population, for a few

days, "ride on Shank's mare.". . .

The house painters of Brooklyn have taken steps to counteract the attempt of the bosses to reduce their wages.

The house carpenters, we are informed, are pretty well "out of the woods" and their demands are generally complied with.

The safe-makers have obtained an increase of wages, and are now at work.

The lithographic printers are making efforts to secure better pay for their labor.

The workmen on the iron clads are yet holding out against the contractors. . . .

The window shade painters have obtained an advance of 25 percent.

The horse shoers are fortifying themselves against the evils of money and trade fluctuations.

The sash and blind-makers are organized and ask their employers for 25 percent additional.

The sugar packers are remodelling their list of prices.

The glass cutters demand 15 percent to present wages.

Imperfect as we confess our list to be, there is enough to convince the reader that the social revolution now working its way through the land must succeed, if workingmen are only true to each other.

The stage drivers, to the number of 800, are on a strike. . . .

The workingmen of Boston are not behind. . . . In addition to the strike at the Charlestown Navy Yard. . . .

The riggers are on a strike. . . .

At this writing it is rumored, says the Boston *Post,* that a general strike is contemplated among the workmen in the iron establishments at South Boston, and other parts of the city.

The war brought many women into shops and factories, often over the objections of men who saw them driving wage scales down. In New York City, girls sewed umbrellas from six in the morning to midnight, earning $3 a week, from which employers deducted the cost of needles and thread. Girls who made cotton shirts received twenty-four cents for a twelve-hour day. In late 1863, New York working women held a mass meeting to find a solution to their problems. A Working Women's Protective Union was formed, and there was a strike of women umbrella workers in New York and Brooklyn. In Providence, Rhode Island, a Ladies Cigar Makers Union was organized.

All together, by 1864, about 200,000 workers, men and women, were in trade unions, forming national unions in some of the trades, putting out labor newspapers.

Union troops were used to break strikes. Federal soldiers were sent to Cold Springs, New York, to end a strike at a gun works where workers wanted a wage increase. Striking machinists and tailors in St. Louis were forced back to work by the army. In Tennessee, a Union general arrested and sent out of the state two hundred striking mechanics. When engineers on the Reading Railroad struck, troops broke that strike, as they did with miners in Tioga County, Pennsylvania.

White workers of the North were not enthusiastic about a war which seemed to be fought for the black slave, or for the capitalist, for anyone but them. They worked in semislave conditions themselves. They thought the war was profiting the new class of millionaires. They saw defective guns sold to the army by contractors, sand sold as sugar, rye sold as coffee, shop sweepings made into clothing and blankets, paper-soled shoes produced for soldiers at the front, navy ships made of rotting timbers, soldiers' uniforms that fell apart in the rain.

The Irish working people of New York, recent immigrants, poor, looked upon with contempt by native Americans, could hardly find sympathy for the black population of the city who competed with them for jobs as longshoremen, barbers, waiters, domestic servants. Blacks, pushed out of these jobs, often were used to break strikes. Then came the war, the draft, the chance of death. And the Conscription Act of 1863 provided that the rich could avoid military service: they could pay $300 or buy a substitute. In the summer of 1863, a "Song of the Conscripts" was circulated by the thousands in New York and other cities. One stanza:

> *We're coming, Father Abraham, three hundred
>   thousand more*
> *We leave our homes and firesides with bleeding
>   hearts and sore*
> *Since poverty has been our crime, we bow to thy
>   decree;*
> *We are the poor and have no wealth to purchase
>   liberty.*

When recruiting for the army began in July 1863, a mob in New York wrecked the main recruiting station. Then, for three days, crowds of white workers marched through the city, destroying buildings, factories, streetcar lines, homes. The draft riots were complex—antiblack, antirich, anti-Republican. From an assault on draft headquarters, the rioters went on to attacks on wealthy homes, then to the murder of blacks. They marched through the streets, forcing factories to close, recruiting more members of the mob. They set the city's colored orphan asylum on fire. They shot, burned, and hanged blacks they found in the streets. Many people were thrown into the rivers to drown.

On the fourth day, Union troops returning from the Battle of Gettysburg came into the city and stopped the rioting. Perhaps four hundred people were killed. No exact figures have ever been given, but the number of lives lost was greater than in any other incident of domestic violence in American history.

Joel Tyler Headley (*The Great Riots of New York*) gave a graphic day-by-day description of what happened:

> Second Day. . . . the fire-bells continually ringing increased the terror that every hour became more widespread. Especially was this true of the negro population. . . . At one time there lay at the corner of Twenty-seventh Street and Seventh Avenue the dead body of a negro, stripped nearly naked, and around it a collection of Irishmen, absolutely dancing or shouting like wild Indians. . . . A ne-

gro barber's shop was next attacked, and the torch
applied to it. A negro lodging house in the same
street next received the visit of these furies, and
was soon a mass of ruins. Old men, seventy years
of age, and young children, too young to compre-
hend what it all meant, were cruelly beaten and
killed. . . .

There were antidraft riots—not so prolonged
or bloody—in other northern cities: Newark, Troy,
Boston, Toledo, Evansville. In Boston the dead were
Irish workers attacking an armory, who were fired
on by soldiers.

In the South, beneath the apparent unity of the
white Confederacy, there was also conflict. Most
whites—two-thirds of them—did not own slaves. A few
thousand families made up the plantation elite. The
Federal Census of 1850 showed that a thousand southern families at the top of the economy received about
$50 million a year income, while all the other families,
about 660,000, received about $60 million a year.

Millions of southern whites were poor farmers,
living in shacks or abandoned outhouses, cultivating
land so bad the plantation owners had abandoned it.
Just before the Civil War, in Jackson, Mississippi, slaves
working in a cotton factory received twenty cents a day
for board, and white workers at the same factory received thirty cents. A newspaper in North Carolina
in August 1855 spoke of "hundreds of thousands of
working class families existing upon half-starvation
from year to year."

Behind the rebel battle yells and the legendary spirit of the Confederate army, there was much

reluctance to fight. A sympathetic historian of the South, E. Merton Coulter, asked: "Why did the Confederacy fail? The forces leading to defeat were many but they may be summed up in this one fact: The people did not will hard enough and long enough to win." Not money or soldiers, but will power and morale were decisive.

The conscription law of the Confederacy too provided that the rich could avoid service. Did Confederate soldiers begin to suspect they were fighting for the privileges of an elite they could never belong to? In April 1863, there was a bread riot in Richmond. That summer, draft riots occurred in various southern cities. In September, a bread riot in Mobile, Alabama. Georgia Lee Tatum, in her study *Disloyalty in the Confederacy,* writes: "Before the end of the war, there was much disaffection in every state, and many of the disloyal had formed into bands—in some states into well-organized, active societies."

The Civil War was one of the first instances in the world of modern warfare: deadly artillery shells, Gatling guns, bayonet charges—combining the indiscriminate killing of mechanized war with hand-to-hand combat. The nightmare scenes could not adequately be described except in a novel like Stephen Crane's *The Red Badge of Courage.* In one charge before Petersburg, Virginia, a regiment of 850 Maine soldiers lost 632 men in half an hour. It was a vast butchery, 623,000 dead on both sides, and 471,000 wounded, over a million dead and wounded in a country whose population was 30 million.

No wonder that desertions grew among southern soldiers as the war went on. As for the Union army, by the end of the war, 200,000 had deserted.

Still, 600,000 had volunteered for the Confederacy in 1861, and many in the Union army were volunteers. The psychology of patriotism, the lure of adventure, the aura of moral crusade created by political leaders, worked effectively to dim class resentments against the rich and powerful, and turn much of the anger against "the enemy." As Edmund Wilson put it in *Patriotic Gore* (written after World War II):

> We have seen, in our most recent wars, how a divided and arguing public opinion may be converted overnight into a national near-unanimity, an obedient flood of energy which will carry the young to destruction and overpower any effort to stem it. The unanimity of men at war is like that of a school of fish, which will swerve, simultaneously and apparently without leadership, when the shadow of an enemy appears, or like a sky-darkening flight of grass-hoppers, which, also all compelled by one impulse, will descend to consume the crops.

Under the deafening noise of the war, Congress was passing and Lincoln was signing into law a whole series of acts to give business interests what they wanted, and what the agrarian South had blocked before secession. The Republican platform of 1860 had been a clear appeal to businessmen. Now Congress in 1861 passed the Morrill Tariff. This made foreign goods more expensive, allowed American manufacturers to raise their prices, and forced American consumers to pay more.

The following year a Homestead Act was passed. It gave 160 acres of western land, unoccupied and publicly owned, to anyone who would cultivate it for five years. Anyone willing to pay $1.25 an acre could buy a homestead. Few ordinary people had the $200 necessary to do this; speculators moved in and bought up much of the land. Homestead land added up to 50 million acres. But during the Civil War, over 100 million acres were given by Congress and the President to various railroads, free of charge. Congress also set up a national bank, putting the government into partnership with the banking interests, guaranteeing their profits.

With strikes spreading, employers pressed Congress for help. The Contract Labor Law of 1864 made it possible for companies to sign contracts with foreign workers whenever the workers pledged to give twelve months of their wages to pay the cost of emigration. This gave the employers during the Civil War not only very cheap labor, but strikebreakers.

More important, perhaps, than the federal laws passed by Congress for the benefit of the rich were the day-to-day operations of local and state laws for the benefit of landlords and merchants. Gustavus Myers, in his *History of the Great American Fortunes*, comments on this in discussing the growth of the Astor family's fortune, much of it out of the rents of New York tenements:

> Is it not murder when, compelled by want, people are forced to fester in squalid, germ-filled tenements, where the sunlight never enters and where

disease finds a prolific breeding-place? Untold
thousands went to their deaths in these unspeak-
able places. Yet, so far as the Law was concerned,
the rents collected by the Astors, as well as by other
landlords, were honestly made. The whole institution of Law saw nothing out of the way in these conditions, and very significantly so, because, to repeat
over and over again, Law did not represent the eth-
ics or ideals of advanced humanity; it exactly reflected, as a pool reflects the sky, the demands and
self-interest of the growing propertied classes. . . .

In the thirty years leading up to the Civil War,
the law was increasingly interpreted in the courts
to suit the capitalist development of the country.
Studying this, Morton Horwitz (*The Transformation
of American Law*) points out that the English common-
law was no longer holy when it stood in the way of
business growth. Mill owners were given the legal
right to destroy other people's property by flood to
carry on their business. The law of "eminent do-
main" was used to take farmers' land and give it to
canal companies or railroad companies as subsidies.
Judgments for damages against businessmen were
taken out of the hands of juries, which were unpredictable, and given to judges. Private settlement of
disputes by arbitration was replaced by court settle-
ments, creating more dependence on lawyers, and
the legal profession gained in importance. The ancient idea of a fair price for goods gave way in the
courts to the idea of caveat emptor (let the buyer be-
ware), thus throwing generations of consumers from
that time on to the mercy of businessmen.

That contract law was intended to discriminate against working people and for business is shown by Horwitz in the following example of the early nineteenth century: the courts said that if a worker signed a contract to work for a year, and left before the year was up, he was not entitled to any wages, even for the time he had worked. But the courts at the same time said that if a building business broke a contract, it was entitled to be paid for whatever had been done up to that point.

The pretense of the law was that a worker and a railroad made a contract with equal bargaining power. Thus, a Massachusetts judge decided an injured worker did not deserve compensation, because, by signing the contract, he was agreeing to take certain risks. "The circle was completed; the law had come simply to ratify those forms of inequality that the market system produced."

It was a time when the law did not even pretend to protect working people—as it would in the next century. Health and safety laws were either nonexistent or unenforced. In Lawrence, Massachusetts, in 1860, on a winter day, the Pemberton Mill collapsed, with nine hundred workers inside, mostly women. Eighty-eight died, and although there was evidence that the structure had never been adequate to support the heavy machinery inside, and that this was known to the construction engineer, a jury found "no evidence of criminal intent."

Horwitz sums up what happened in the courts of law by the time of the Civil War:

> By the middle of the nineteenth century the le-
> gal system had been reshaped to the advantage of
> men of commerce and industry at the expense of
> farmers, workers, consumers, and other less pow-
> erful groups within the society. . . . it actively pro-
> moted a legal redistribution of wealth against the
> weakest groups in the society.

In premodern times, the maldistribution of
wealth was accomplished by simple force. In modern
times, exploitation is disguised—it is accomplished
by law, which has the look of neutrality and fairness.
By the time of the Civil War, modernization was well
under way in the United States.

With the war over, the urgency of national unity
slackened, and ordinary people could turn more to
their daily lives, their problems of survival. The dis-
banded armies now were in the streets, looking for
work. In June 1865, *Fincher's Trades' Review* reported:
"As was to be expected, the returned soldiers are flood-
ing the streets already, unable to find employment."

The cities to which the soldiers returned were
death traps of typhus, tuberculosis, hunger, and
fire. In New York, 100,000 people lived in the cellars of the slums; 12,000 women worked in houses
of prostitution to keep from starving; the garbage,
lying 2 feet deep in the streets, was alive with rats.
In Philadelphia, while the rich got fresh water from
the Schuylkill River, everyone else drank from the
Delaware, into which 13 million gallons of sewage
were dumped every day. In the Great Chicago Fire
in 1871, the tenements fell so fast, one after another,
that people said it sounded like an earthquake.

A movement for the eight-hour day began among working people after the war, helped by the formation of the first national federation of unions, the National Labor Union. A three-month strike of 100,000 workers in New York won the eight-hour day, and at a victory celebration in June 1872, 150,000 workers paraded through the city. The *New York Times* wondered what proportion of the strikers were "thoroughly American."

Women, brought into industry during the war, organized unions: cigarmakers, tailoresses, umbrella sewers, capmakers, printers, laundresses, shoeworkers. They formed the Daughters of St. Crispin, and succeeded in getting the Cigarmakers Union and the National Typographical Union to admit women for the first time. A woman named Gussie Lewis of New York became corresponding secretary of the Typographers' Union. But the cigarmakers and typographers were only two of the thirty-odd national unions, and the general attitude toward women was one of exclusion.

In 1869, the collar laundresses of Troy, New York, whose work involved standing "over the wash tub and over the ironing table with furnaces on either side, the thermometer averaging 100 degrees, for wages averaging $2.00 and $3.00 a week" (according to a contemporary account), went on strike. Their leader was Kate Mullaney, second vice-president of the National Labor Union. Seven thousand people came to a rally to support them, and the women organized a cooperative collar and cuff factory to provide work and keep the strike going. But as time went on, outside support dwindled. The employers began mak-

ing a paper collar, requiring fewer laundresses. The
strike failed.

The dangers of mill work intensified efforts to
organize. Work often went on around the clock. At
a mill in Providence, Rhode Island, fire broke out
one night in 1866. There was panic among the six
hundred workers, mostly women, and many jumped
to their deaths from upper-story windows.

In Fall River, Massachusetts, women weavers
formed a union independent of the men weavers.
They refused to take a 10 percent wage cut that the
men had accepted, struck against three mills, won
the men's support, and brought to a halt 3,500 looms
and 156,000 spindles, with 3,200 workers on strike.
But their children needed food; they had to return
to work, signing an "iron-clad oath" (later called a
"yellow-dog contract") not to join a union.

Black workers at this time found the National
Labor Union reluctant to organize them. So they
formed their own unions and carried on their own
strikes—like the levee workers in Mobile, Alabama,
in 1867, Negro longshoremen in Charleston, dock-
workers in Savannah. This probably stimulated the
National Labor Union, at its 1869 convention, to re-
solve to organize women and Negroes, declaring that
it recognized "neither color nor sex on the question
of the rights of labor." A journalist wrote about the
remarkable signs of racial unity at this convention:

> When a native Mississippian and an ex-confederate
> officer, in addressing a convention, refers to a col-
> ored delegate who has preceded him as "the gentle-
> man from Georgia" . . . when an ardent and Dem-

ocratic partisan (from New York at that) declares
with a rich Irish brogue that he asks for himself
no privilege as a mechanic or as a citizen that he is
not willing to concede to every other man, white or
black . . . then one may indeed be warranted in asserting that time works curious changes. . . .

Most unions, however, still kept Negroes out, or
asked them to form their own locals.

The National Labor Union began to expend
more and more of its energy on political issues, especially currency reform, a demand for the issuance
of paper money: Greenbacks. As it became less an
organizer of labor struggles, and more a lobbyist
with Congress, concerned with voting, it lost vitality.
An observer of the labor scene, F. A. Sorge, wrote in
1870 to Karl Marx in England: "The National Labor
Union, which had such brilliant prospects in the beginning of its career, was poisoned by Greenbackism
and is slowly but surely dying."

Perhaps unions could not easily see the limits to
legislative reform in an age where such reform laws
were being passed for the first time, and hopes were
high. The Pennsylvania legislature in 1869 passed
a mine safety act providing for the "regulation and
ventilation of mines, and for the protection of the
lives of the miners." Only after a hundred years of
continuing accidents in those mines would it be understood how insufficient those words were—except
as a device to calm anger among miners.

In 1873, another economic crisis devastated the
nation. It was the closing of the banking house of Jay
Cooke—the banker who during the war had made

$3 million a year in commissions alone for selling government bonds—that started the wave of panic. While President Grant slept in Cooke's Philadelphia mansion on September 18, 1873, the banker rode downtown to lock the door on his bank. Now people could not pay loans on mortgages: five thousand businesses closed and put their workers on the street.

It was more than Jay Cooke. The crisis was built into a system which was chaotic in its nature, in which only the very rich were secure. It was a system of periodic crisis—1837, 1857, 1873 (and later: 1893, 1907, 1919, 1929)—that wiped out small businesses and brought cold, hunger, and death to working people while the fortunes of the Astors, Vanderbilts, Rockefellers, Morgans, kept growing through war and peace, crisis and recovery. During the 1873 crisis, Carnegie was capturing the steel market, Rockefeller was wiping out his competitors in oil.

"LABOR DEPRESSION IN BROOKLYN" was the headline in the New York *Herald* in November 1873. It listed closings and layoffs: a felt-skirt factory, a picture-frame factory, a glass-cutting establishment, a steelworks factory. And women's trades: milliners, dressmakers, shoe-binders.

The depression continued through the 1870s. During the first three months of 1874, ninety thousand workers, almost half of them women, had to sleep in police stations in New York. They were known as "revolvers" because they were limited to one or two days a month in any one police station, and so had to keep moving. All over the country, people were evicted from their homes. Many roamed the cities looking for food.

Desperate workers tried to get to Europe or to South America. In 1878, the SS *Metropolis*, filled with laborers, left the United States for South America and sank with all aboard. The New York *Tribune* reported: "One hour after the news that the ship had gone down arrived in Philadelphia, the office of Messrs. Collins was besieged by hundreds of hunger-bitten, decent men, begging for the places of the drowned laborers."

Mass meeting and demonstrations of the unemployed took place all over the country. Unemployed councils were set up. A meeting in New York at Cooper Institute in late 1873, organized by trade unions and the American section of the First International (founded in 1864 in Europe by Marx and others), drew a huge crowd, overflowing into the streets. The meeting asked that before bills became law they should be approved by a public vote, that no individual should own more than $30,000; they asked for an eight-hour day. Also:

> Whereas, we are industrious, law-abiding citizens, who had paid all taxes and given support and allegiance to the government,
>
> Resolved, that we will in this time of need supply ourselves and our families with proper food and shelter and we will send our bills to the City Treasury, to be liquidated, until we shall obtain work. . . .

In Chicago, twenty thousand unemployed marched through the streets to City Hall asking "bread for the needy, clothing for the naked, and

houses for the homeless." Actions like this resulted
in some relief for about ten thousand families.

In January 1874, in New York City, a huge parade of workers, kept by the police from approach-
ing City Hall, went to Tompkins Square, and there
were told by the police they couldn't have the meeting. They stayed, and the police attacked. One newspaper reported:

> Police clubs rose and fell. Women and children
> ran screaming in all directions. Many of them
> were trampled underfoot in the stampede for the
> gates. In the street bystanders were ridden down
> and mercilessly clubbed by mounted officers.

Strikes were called in the textile mills of Fall
River, Massachusetts. In the anthracite coal district
of Pennsylvania, there was the "long strike," where
Irish members of a society called the Ancient Order of Hibernians were accused of acts of violence,
mostly on the testimony of a detective planted among
the miners. These were the "Molly Maguires." They
were tried and found guilty. Philip Foner believes,
after a study of the evidence, that they were framed
because they were labor organizers. He quotes the
sympathetic *Irish World*, which called them "intelli-
gent men whose direction gave strength to the resistance of the miners to the inhuman reduction of
their wages." And he points to the *Miners' Journal*,
put out by the coal mine owners, which referred
to the executed men this way: "What did they do?
Whenever prices of labor did not suit them they organized and proclaimed a strike."

All together, nineteen were executed, according to Anthony Bimba (*The Molly Maguires*). There were scattered protests from workingmen's organizations, but no mass movement that could stop the executions.

It was a time when employers brought in recent immigrants—desperate for work, different from the strikers in language and culture—to break strikes. Italians were imported into the bituminous coal area around Pittsburgh in 1874 to replace striking miners. This led to the killing of three Italians, to trials in which jurors of the community exonerated the strikers, and bitter feelings between Italians and other organized workers.

The centennial year of 1876—one hundred years after the Declaration of Independence—brought forth a number of new declarations (reproduced by Philip Foner in *We the Other People*). Whites and blacks, separately, expressed their disillusionment. A "Negro Declaration of Independence" denounced the Republican party on which they had once depended to gain full freedom, and proposed independent political action by colored voters. And the Workingmen's party of Illinois, at a July 4 celebration organized by German socialists in Chicago, said in its Declaration of Independence:

> The present system has enabled capitalists to make laws in their own interests to the injury and oppression of the workers.
>
> It has made the name Democracy, for which our forefathers fought and died, a mockery and a shadow, by giving to property an unproportionate

amount of representation and control over Legislation.

It has enabled capitalists . . . to secure government aid, inland grants and money loans, to selfish railroad corporations, who, by monopolizing
the means of transportation are enabled to swin-
dle both the producer and the consumer. . . .

It has presented to the world the absurd spec-
tacle of a deadly civil war for the abolition of negro slavery while the majority of the white population, those who have created all the wealth of the
nation, are compelled to suffer under a bondage
infinitely more galling and humiliating. . . .

It has allowed the capitalists, as a class, to appropriate annually 5/6 of the entire production of
the country. . . .

It has therefore prevented mankind from ful-
filling their natural destinies on earth—crushed
out ambition, prevented marriages or caused false
and unnatural ones—has shortened human life,
destroyed morals and fostered crime, corrupted
judges, ministers, and statesmen, shattered confidence, love and honor among men, and made life
a selfish, merciless struggle for existence instead
of a noble and generous struggle for perfection,
in which equal advantages should be given to all,
and human lives relieved from an unnatural and
degrading competition for bread. . . .

We, therefore, the representatives of the workers of Chicago, in mass meeting assembled, do sol-
emnly publish and declare. . .

That we are absolved from all allegiance to
the existing political parties of this country, and

that as free and independent producers we shall
endeavor to acquire the full power to make our
own laws, manage our own production, and govern ourselves, acknowledging no rights without
duties, no duties without rights. And for the support of this declaration, with a firm reliance on
the assistance and cooperation of all workingmen,
we mutually pledge to each other our lives, our
means, and our sacred honor.

In the year 1877, the country was in the depths of
the Depression. That summer, in the hot cities where
poor families lived in cellars and drank infested water, the children became sick in large numbers. The
New York Times wrote: " . . . already the cry of the dying children begins to be heard. . . . Soon, to judge
from the past, there will be a thousand deaths of
infants per week in the city." That first week in July,
in Baltimore, where all liquid sewage ran through
the streets, 139 babies died.

That year there came a series of tumultuous
strikes by railroad workers in a dozen cities; they
shook the nation as no labor conflict in its history
had done.

It began with wage cuts on railroad after railroad, in tense situations of already low wages ($1.75
a day for brakemen working twelve hours), scheming
and profiteering by the railroad companies, deaths
and injuries among the workers—loss of hands, feet,
fingers, the crushing of men between cars.

At the Baltimore & Ohio station in Martinsburg,
West Virginia, workers determined to fight the
wage cut went on strike, uncoupled the engines, ran

them into the roundhouse, and announced no more
trains would leave Martinsburg until the 10 percent
cut was canceled. A crowd of support gathered, too
many for the local police to disperse. B. & O. officials asked the governor for military protection, and
he sent in militia. A train tried to get through, protected by the militia, and a striker, trying to derail
it, exchanged gunfire with a militiaman attempting
to stop him. The striker was shot in his thigh and
his arm. His arm was amputated later that day, and
nine days later he died.

Six hundred freight trains now jammed the
yards at Martinsburg. The West Virginia governor
applied to newly elected President Rutherford Hayes
for federal troops, saying the state militia was insufficient. In fact, the militia was not totally reliable, being composed of many railroad workers. Much of the
U.S. army was tied up in Indian battles in the West.
Congress had not appropriated money for the army
yet, but J. P. Morgan, August Belmont, and other
bankers now offered to lend money to pay army officers (but no enlisted men). Federal troops arrived
in Martinsburg, and the freight cars began to move.

In Baltimore, a crowd of thousands sympathetic
to the railroad strikers surrounded the armory of
the National Guard, which had been called out by
the governor at the request of the B. & O. Railroad.
The crowd hurled rocks, and the soldiers came out,
firing. The streets now became the scene of a moving, bloody battle. When the evening was over, ten
men or boys were dead, more badly wounded, one
soldier wounded. Half of the 120 troops quit and
the rest went on to the train depot, where a crowd

of two hundred smashed the engine of a passenger train, tore up tracks, and engaged the militia again in a running battle.

By now, fifteen thousand people surrounded the depot. Soon, three passenger cars, the station platform, and a locomotive were on fire. The governor asked for federal troops, and Hayes responded. Five hundred soldiers arrived and Baltimore quieted down.

The rebellion of the railroad workers now spread. Joseph Dacus, then editor of the St. Louis *Republican*, reported:

> Strikes were occurring almost every hour. The great State of Pennsylvania was in an uproar; New Jersey was afflicted by a paralyzing dread; New York was mustering an army of militia; Ohio was shaken from Lake Erie to the Ohio River; Indiana rested in a dreadful suspense. Illinois, and especially its great metropolis, Chicago, apparently hung on the verge of a vortex of confusion and tumult. St. Louis had already felt the effect of the premonitory shocks of the uprising. . . .

The strike spread to Pittsburgh and the Pennsylvania Railroad. Again, it happened outside the regular union, pent-up anger exploding without plan. Robert Bruce, historian of the 1877 strikes, writes *(1877: Year of Violence)* about a flagman named Gus Harris. Harris refused to go out on a "double-header," a train with two locomotives carrying a double length of cars, to which railroaders had objected because it required fewer workers and made the brakemen's work more dangerous:

The decision was his own, not part of a concerted plan or a general understanding. Had he lain awake that past night, listening to the rain, asking himself if he dared quit, wondering if anyone would join him, weighing the chances? Or had he simply risen to a breakfast that did not fill him, seen his children go off shabby and half-fed, walked brooding through the damp morning and then yielded impulsively to stored-up rage?

When Harris said he would not go, the rest of the crew refused too. The strikers now multiplied, joined by young boys and men from the mills and factories (Pittsburgh had 33 iron mills, 73 glass factories, 29 oil refineries, 158 coal mines). The freight trains stopped moving out of the city. The Trainman's Union had not organized this, but it moved to take hold, called a meeting, invited "all workingmen to make common cause with their brethren on the railroad."

Railroad and local officials decided that the Pittsburgh militia would not kill their fellow townsmen, and urged that Philadelphia troops be called in. By now two thousand cars were idle in Pittsburgh. The Philadelphia troops came and began to clear the track. Rocks flew. Gunfire was exchanged between crowd and troops. At least ten people were killed, all workingmen, most of them not railroaders.

Now the whole city rose in anger. A crowd surrounded the troops, who moved into a roundhouse. Railroad cars were set afire, buildings began to burn, and finally the roundhouse itself, the troops marching out of it to safety. There was more gunfire, the Union Depot was set afire, thousands looted the freight cars. A huge grain elevator and a small section of the city went up in flames. In a few days, twenty-four people had been killed (including four soldiers). Seventy-nine buildings had been burned to the ground. Something like a general strike was developing in Pittsburgh: mill workers, car workers, miners, laborers, and the employees at the Carnegie steel plant.

The entire National Guard of Pennsylvania, nine thousand men, was called out. But many of the companies couldn't move as strikers in other towns held up traffic. In Lebanon, Pennsylvania, one National Guard company mutinied and marched through an excited town. In Altoona, troops surrounded by rioters, immobilized by sabotaged engines, surrendered, stacked arms, fraternized with the crowd, and then were allowed to go home, to the accompaniment of singing by a quartet in an all-Negro militia company.

In Harrisburg, the state capital, as at so many places, teenagers made up a large part of the crowd, which included some Negroes. Philadelphia militia, on their way home from Altoona, shook hands with the crowd, gave up their guns, marched like captives through the streets, were fed at a hotel and sent home. The crowd agreed to the mayor's request to deposit the surrendered guns at the city hall. Factories and shops were idle. After some looting, citizens' patrols kept order in the streets through the night.

Where strikers did not manage to take control, as in Pottsville, Pennsylvania, it may well have been because of disunity. The spokesman of the Philadelphia & Reading Coal & Iron Company in that town wrote: "The men have no organization, and there is too much race jealousy existing among them to permit them to form one."

In Reading, Pennsylvania, there was no such problem—90 percent were native-born, the rest mostly German. There, the railroad was two months behind in paying wages, and a branch of the Trainman's Union was organized. Two thousand people gathered, while men who had blackened their faces with coal dust set about methodically tearing up tracks, jamming switches, derailing cars, setting fire to cabooses and also to a railroad bridge.

A National Guard company arrived, fresh from duty at the execution of the Molly Maguires. The crowd threw stones, fired pistols. The soldiers fired into the crowd. "Six men lay dead in the twilight," Bruce reports, "a fireman and an engineer formerly employed in the Reading, a carpenter, a huckster, a rolling-mill worker, a laborer. . . . A policeman and another man lay at the point of death." Five of the wounded died. The crowd grew angrier, more menacing. A contingent of soldiers announced it would not fire, one soldier saying he would rather put a bullet through the president of Philadelphia & Reading Coal & Iron. The 16th Regiment of the Morristown volunteers stacked its arms. Some militia threw their guns away and gave their ammunition to the crowd. When the Guardsmen left for home, federal troops arrived and took control, and local police began making arrests.

Meanwhile the leaders of the big railway brotherhoods, the Order of Railway Conductors, the Brotherhood of Locomotive Firemen, the Brotherhood of Engineers, disavowed the strike. There was talk in the press of "communistic ideas . . . widely entertained . . . by the workmen employed in mines and factories and by the railroads."

In fact, there was a very active Workingmen's party in Chicago, with several thousand members, most of them immigrants from Germany and Bohemia. It was connected with the First International in Europe. In the midst of the railroad strikes, that summer of 1877, it called a rally. Six thousand people came and demanded nationalization of the railroads. Albert Parsons gave a fiery speech. He was from Alabama, had fought in the Confederacy during the Civil War, married a brown-skinned woman of Spanish and Indian blood, worked as a typesetter, and was one of the best English-speaking orators the Workingmen's party had.

The next day, a crowd of young people, not especially connected with the rally of the evening before, began moving through the railroad yards, closed down the freights, went to the factories, called out the mill workers, the stockyard workers, the crewmen on the Lake Michigan ships, closed down the brickyards and lumberyards. That day also, Albert Parsons was fired from his job with the Chicago *Times* and declared blacklisted.

The police attacked the crowds. The press reported: "The sound of clubs falling on skulls was sickening for the first minute, until one grew accustomed to it. A rioter dropped at every whack, it seemed, for the ground was covered with them." Two companies of U.S. infantry arrived, joining National Guardsmen and Civil War veterans. Police fired into a surging crowd, and three men were killed.

The next day, an armed crowd of five thousand fought the police. The police fired again and again, and when it was over, and the dead were counted, they were, as usual, workingmen and boys, eighteen of them, their skulls smashed by clubs, their vital organs pierced by gunfire.

The one city where the Workingmen's party clearly led the rebellion was St. Louis, a city of flour mills, foundries, packing houses, machine shops, breweries, and railroads. Here, as elsewhere, there were wage cuts on the railroads. And here there were perhaps a thousand members of the Workingmen's party, many of them bakers, coopers, cabinetmakers, cigarmakers, brewery workers. The party was organized in four sections, by nationality: German, English, French, Bohemian.

All four sections took a ferry across the Mississippi to join a mass meeting of railroad men in East St. Louis. One of their speakers told the meeting: "All you have to do, gentlemen, for you have the numbers, is to unite on one idea—that the workingmen shall rule the country. What man makes, belongs to him, and the workingmen made this country." Railroaders in East St. Louis declared themselves on strike. The mayor of East St. Louis was a European immigrant, himself an active revolutionist as a youth, and railroad men's votes dominated the city.

In St. Louis, itself, the Workingmen's party called an open-air mass meeting to which five thousand people came. The party was clearly in the leadership of the strike. Speakers, excited by the crowd, became more militant: " . . . capital has changed liberty into serfdom, and we must fight or die." They called for nationalization of the railroads, mines, and all industry.

At another huge meeting of the Workingmen's party a black man spoke for those who worked on the steamboats and levees. He asked: "Will you stand to us regardless of color?" The crowd shouted back: "We will!" An executive committee was set up, and it called for a general strike of all branches of industry in St. Louis.

Handbills for the general strike were soon all over the city. There was a march of four hundred Negro steamboat men and roustabouts along the river, six hundred factory workers carrying a banner: "No Monopoly—Workingmen's Rights." A great procession moved through the city, ending with a rally of ten thousand people listening to Communist speakers: "The people are rising up in their might and declaring they will no longer submit to being oppressed by unproductive capital."

David Burbank, in his book on the St. Louis events, *Reign of the Rabble,* writes:

> Only around St. Louis did the original strike on the railroads expand into such a systematically organized and complete shut-down of all industry that the term general strike is fully justified. And only there did the socialists assume undisputed leadership. . . . no American city has come so close to being ruled by a workers' soviet, as we would now call it, as St. Louis, Missouri, in the year 1877.

The railroad strikes were making news in Europe. Marx wrote Engels: "What do you think of the workers of the United States? This first explosion against the associated oligarchy of capital which has occurred since the Civil War will naturally again be suppressed, but can very well form the point of origin of an earnest workers' party. . . ."

In New York, several thousand gathered at Tompkins Square. The tone of the meeting was moderate, speaking of "a political revolution through the ballot box." And: "If you will unite, we may have here within five years a socialistic republic. . . . Then will a lovely morning break over this darkened land." It was a peaceful meeting. It adjourned. The last words heard from the platform were: "Whatever we poor men may not have, we have free speech, and no one can take it from us." Then the police charged, using their clubs.

In St. Louis, as elsewhere, the momentum of the crowds, the meetings, the enthusiasm, could not be sustained. As they diminished, the police, militia, and federal troops moved in and the authorities took over. The police raided the headquarters of the Workingmen's party and arrested seventy people; the executive committee that had been for a while virtually in charge of the city was now in prison. The strikers surrendered; the wage cuts remained; 131 strike leaders were fired by the Burlington Railroad.

When the great railroad strikes of 1877 were over, a hundred people were dead, a thousand people had gone to jail, 100,000 workers had gone on strike, and the strikes had roused into action countless unemployed in the cities. More than half the freight on the nation's 75,000 miles of track had stopped running at the height of the strikes.

The railroads made some concessions, withdrew some wage cuts, but also strengthened their "Coal and Iron Police." In a number of large cities, National Guard armories were built, with loopholes for guns. Robert Bruce believes the strikes taught many people of the hardships of others, and that they led to congressional railroad regulation. They may have stimulated the business unionism of the American Federation of Labor as well as the national unity of labor proposed by the Knights of Labor, and the independent labor-farmer parties of the next two decades.

In 1877, the same year blacks learned they did not have enough strength to make real the promise of equality in the Civil War, working people learned they were not united enough, not powerful enough, to defeat the combination of private capital and government power. But there was more to come.

BOOKS BY HOWARD ZINN

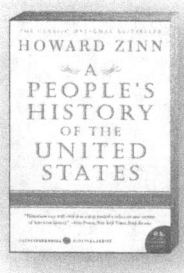